A-Z Colour Guide to
HOMEMAKING CRAFTS

MI

A-Z Colour Guide to
HOMEMAKING CRAFTS

Marie Katherine Burne-Jones

LANGHAM PRESS

First published in 1983 by Langham Press,
Langham Park, Catteshall Lane,
Godalming, Surrey
in association with Octopus Books Limited,
59 Grosvenor Street, London W1

© 1983 Octopus Books Limited
ISBN 0 86362 002 7

Printed in Hong Kong

CONTENTS

A-Z OF HOMEMAKING CRAFTS   6

SUPPLIERS   124

INDEX   126

Acknowledgements

The Publishers wish to thank the following individuals and organisations for their kind permission to reproduce the pictures in this book.

Bryce Atwell, 107; Michael Boys, 11; Camera Press, 102; The Designers Guild, 34, 38–39, 62–63, 110; International Press Services Ltd, 22; Val Jackson, 42; Living Magazine, 70, 83, 90, 90–91; Bill Mclaughlin, 10, 15, 47, 50, 63, 114; Jessica Strang, 93; Sunway Blinds, 14 top left; Syndication International, 95; Transworld Features Syndicate UK 1 TD.

APPLIQUÉ

Appliqué is the technique of applying or stitching pieces of fabric on to a background fabric either by hand or machine. Different effects can be achieved with various fabrics to create areas of contrast or harmony. Motifs can be applied at random, as a repeat pattern, in a small section or panel.

Appliqué can be used for practical items such as bedspreads, linen and curtains as well as to decorate clothes or make pictures. Choose fruit, flower or vegetable shapes for the kitchen, shells, fish or rainbows for a bathroom and perhaps animals, trains, clouds or nursery characters for a child's room.

Fabrics

The background fabric as well as the applied fabric should be closely woven and unlikely to fray. Felt is a good choice for beginners as it is easy to cut, will not fray and can be stitched directly to the background. If you want to use a flimsy fabric, back it first with an iron-on interfacing to strengthen it.

Bear in mind the use of the article. Choose fabrics which are preshrunk (or wash them first) and colour-fast. Consider how often the article must be washed and make sure the appliqué matches the properties of the background fabric.

Different methods

There are two ways to apply appliqué. One is to use shapes with raw edges so that the edges are totally or partially covered by stitches to prevent fraying. The other way is to apply shapes with turned edges. The basic procedure is the same for both methods.

Raw edge appliqué

Cut the shape to the exact size you want using a paper pattern or template. You can cut it freehand if you are confident and are aiming for a fairly free-form design.

Pin motif to background fabric and baste it securely. Cover the raw edge completely with a line of closely worked machine or handsewn satin stitch. This line of stitches will prevent fraying as well as attaching the motif to your background fabric.

Alternatively, you can use a machine ZIGZAG STITCH or handsewn buttonhole stitch. These methods are most suitable for non-fraying fabrics or for an article that will not need much washing, such as a bedspread.

You can also choose from a range of decorative stitches such as HERRINGBONE or CHAIN STITCH. It is best to use these only where it will enhance the look of the finished article.

Turned edge appliqué

Cut out your motifs, but this time allow an extra 5mm (¼in) all round for turnings. Allowances can be turned under by hand or pressed. There are two ways of applying turned-edge appliqué – both will need pinning to the background fabric.

The first method involves securing the shapes on to the background and turning the edges as the work progresses. You can use a stitch-ripper to turn in the fabric, sliding it under the folded edge and pinning as you go. Alternatively, you can turn in the edges and tack before securing the motif to the background. Avoid using bright thread for tacking as this may mark a pale background.

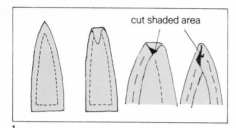

cut shaded area

1

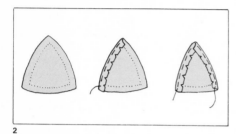

2

When using turned-edge appliqué you will have to turn in corners. For a neat finish these should be mitred and any curved edges will need clipping so that they will lie flat.

1 For sharp corners of 45° or less, turn the point over first, then turn in each of the sides. Tack using small stitches.

2 For a wider angled corner, turn in the left hand side, then the right hand side and, again, tack with small stitches. Only trim the turning if the fabric is thick.

Padded appliqué

You will need to cut the motif a little larger to allow for padding. Also allow 5mm (¼in) for a turning. Turn back raw edges and pin or tack to background fabric. Oversew motif to background with small stitches, leaving an opening for the wadding. Insert wadding and push into place with a pencil or wooden spoon. Sew up opening.

Bonding

For quick results, your appliqué motifs can be bonded to the background. The bonding material is a non-woven adhesive web prepared with a special paper backing.

Cut a piece of bonding that is slightly larger than your motif. Draw the outline of the shape on to the paper backing and iron on to the wrong side of the motif. Allow to cool and cut out the motif shape. Peel off the paper and place the motif, right side up, on to the background and iron in position.

You can still add a decorative stitch either by hand or machine round the edge if you wish.

BACKSTITCH

This is a useful stitch to use where machine stitching might be too obvious. The stitches should be small and even, and will be strong enough to use for seams. On the right side of the fabric they will look very much like machine stitching, and on the wrong side the stitches will overlap.

Start with a double stitch on the right side. Take a small stitch then insert the needle about 3mm (⅛in)

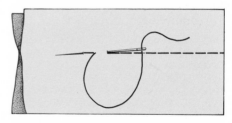

back and bring the point out 3mm forward on the seam line. Keep inserting the needle in the end of the last stitch and bring the point up one stitch ahead.

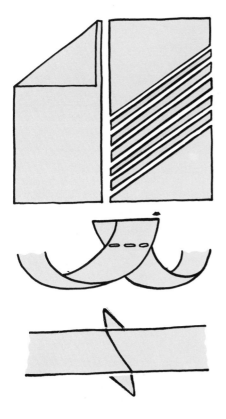

BIAS BINDING

Bias binding is a strip of fabric cut on the true bias of the fabric and is used as a decorative edge or to bind raw edges.

Bias binding is available in a wide range of colours and widths, but is usually made of plain cotton or a synthetic material with a matt surface. If you prefer you can make your own from the same fabric as the main article or in a contrasting fabric.

The main advantage of bias binding is that it can stretch and will bind round corners without puckering.

1 First fold the fabric on the true grain, that is from corner to corner diagonally

so that one selvedge is at right angles to the other selvedge.

2 Cut along the fold line and then cut 2.5cm (1in) strips parallel to the first cutting line. The strips can be as wide as you like, but for ordinary edge binding 2.5cm is ideal.

3 Place the strips with right sides facing and raw edges matching. Pin, tack and then machine stitch 1.5cm (½in) in from the edge.

4 Unfold the strip and trim off the points. Press lightly.

When attaching binding to the raw edge, place the pins at right angles to prevent the tape slipping as you sew. This is particularly important if you have to sew round corners.

BLANKET STITCH

Like HERRINGBONE STITCH, this is a useful stitch for finishing raw edges and it is often used for decoratively attached APPLIQUÉ motifs (see pages 7–8). It can also be used on non-fraying edges such as felt or leather.

Working from left to right, insert the needle into the fabric about 5mm (¼in) down from the edge. Hold the needle

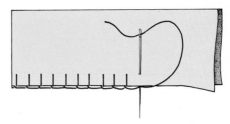

vertically and let the thread run under the needle to form a loop stitch. The thread will run horizontally along the edge of the fabric until you insert the needle for the next stitch.

Above: An attractive solution to an awkward shaped window recess. A colourful blind that drapes comfortably behind a length of wooden dowelling to show off the shape of the window.

Left: Bold flower motifs make a cheerful covering for this sunny bay window.

BLINDS

Blinds are a simple and decorative way to shade a window or to conceal an unattractive view. You can buy ready-made blinds in a wide range of sizes and fabrics, or bamboos, but you may prefer to make your own to suit a particular shape of window or to match up with other furnishings.

Decide whether you want your blind positioned inside or outside the window recess. If it is to hang inside, you will need to measure the height and width from recess to recess. If it is to hang outside the window frame, allow 10cm (4in) each side and at the top and bottom. Directions for measuring windows for making curtains (see page 30) will help.

Types of fabric

Linen, canvas and glazed cottons are the most suitable fabrics for making blinds. There is also a wide range of PVC coated fabrics which are ideal for blinds in kitchens and bathrooms. They are not affected by steam and can easily be wiped clean.

The fabric you buy will need to be the length of your window plus 10cm (4in) for hems. If your window is wider than the fabric, you will need to buy two widths and join them using a FLAT AND FELL SEAM.

Roller blinds

Most department stores, craft and good hardware shops sell roller blind kits. They are usually available in various sizes graduating by 30cm (12in). Unless your window is the exact size of one of the kits, you will need to buy the next size up and cut it back to fit.

Each kit contains a wooden roller, fitted at one end with a spring; a round metal cap which fits over the other end; two wall brackets, one with a hole into which you slot the spring end and one already slotted; a wooden batten to weight down the blind; a length of cord and a pull, screws and tacks. You may have to buy screws separately for fixing the brackets to the wall.

Preparing the fabric

1 Unless the blind is exactly the right size, cut to the required width. The width of the fabric should be the same as the wooden part of the roller with 4cm (1½in) added. Turn in the side edges 1.5cm (½in) and then a further 2.5cm (1in). The material will now be slightly less than the width of the roller to allow for the space taken up once the metal ends are in position. Machine or hand sew these hems.

Turn up the bottom hem 1.5cm (½in) and then turn up again to allow an opening wide enough to slide in the batten. Machine stitch across width but leave ends open. Cut batten to

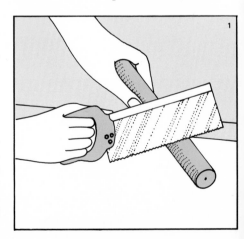

1.5cm (½in) shorter than width of blind. Slide batten into opening and sew both ends to keep batten secure inside hem.

2 Place the blind on a flat surface, right side of fabric up. Press a 1.5cm (½in) hem at the top, right side of fabric to right side. With the spring side of the roller on the left, place roller to top of blind and hammer in the tacks. The roller should have a straight line marked on it for guidance. This is important or else the blind will be slanted and will not roll up or hang properly. Replace metal cap on end of roller.

Take the supplied length of cord for the pull and, with a knot in one end, thread it through the widest part of the 'acorn'. Now thread cord through the cord holder from the domed side and make another knot. Screw cord holder to middle of batten, on the wrong side of the blind. Put acorn's cap on when you have decided on the right length of the cord.

3 Place brackets in position on the wall, inside or outside the recess, as already decided. Carefully rest blind in position in brackets. Pull blind up and down a couple of times to check that it runs freely.

Shaped hems
To give a fancy touch to your blind, you may want to add a scalloped or shaped hem to go below the batten. This should be incorporated into the blind before you add the batten.

First cut a piece of paper the width of your batten and 15cm (6in) deep. Fold the paper in half to find the exact centre. Draw the design you want on the paper. You can trace an outline from a book of stencils, or choose a shape that is complementary to the pattern on the blind. Draw the design on the paper while it is still folded in half and cut around the outline.

Cut a length of fabric that is 15cm (6 in) deep and 2cm (¾in) wider than your blind. If you are using a light fabric it will hang better if it is interfaced. Iron interfacing on to fabric. Pin facing fabric, stiffened side up, to the bottom edge of hem on the

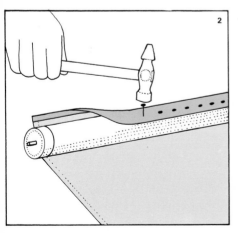

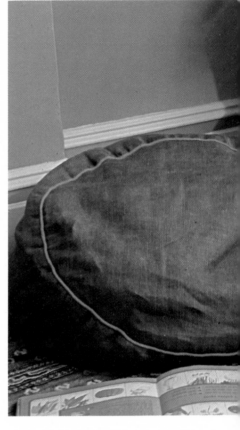

right side of the blind. Pin your pattern on to double fabric and cut out. Machine facing to blind 5mm (¼in) in from cut edge. Cut any curves or angles and turn facing to wrong side of blind. Turn in the side edges of the facing and SLIPSTITCH to blind.

Now turn under the top 5mm (¼in) of facing and machine to the blind. Machine another row of stitches 2.5cm (1in) below to make a casing for the batten.

BOLSTERS

Bolsters are used as supportive bed cushions behind the pillows or as an alternative shape for a scatter CUSH-ION. The same basic pattern can be used larger, with a filling of poly-styrene granules, to make sag bags.

Fabric

For the ends of the bolster you will need two circles of fabric measured to the required diameter, plus 3cm

(1¼in). The main section will take a rectangle of fabric, the same width as the circumference of the ends, plus 3cm (1¼in) for short sides, and the length of the bolster plus 3cm.

Making up the bolster

First make a line of marking stitches approx 1.5cm (½in) in from the edge at both short sides of the main piece of fabric. Snip into these edges up to the line of stitching at equal intervals.

With right sides of the fabric to-gether, pin one of the snipped edges to

one of the circles. As you do this you will find that the snips open out. Pin, tack and stitch the long edges together for 2.5cm (1in) at one end where they meet, parallel to the raw edge. Press the seams open and neaten edges.

Fit the other snipped end of the main section to the second circle in the same way. Tack, then machine stitch round both ends with the snipped edges uppermost in your machine. Trim the edges close to the stitching. Turn the bolster cover right side out and sew up the opening.

Sag bags

Make up an inner casing, but leave an opening that is large enough to insert a cardboard tube. Tie the opening of the bag of granules round one end of the tube and insert the other into the opening of the casing. Pour the granules down the tube until the casing is three-quarters full. Remove the tube and sew up the opening securely, particularly if children will be playing on them. Make the main cover as described above, but leave a bigger opening to insert the granules.

15

BORDERS

Borders are used to add a decorative finish to a rug, quilt, or any soft furnishing that needs a tidy edge.

1 First cut strips approx 5cm (2in) wide for all four sides. Pin one strip along each edge with an overhang of fabric equal to the width of the strip.

2 Machine first strip in position. Fold back fabric and then machine second strip, taking stitching as far as bottom of first strip to form a corner.

3 To MITRE the corners, fold one strip against the other, right sides together and raw edges matching. Machine as shown to form an angle of 90°.

4 Trim excess fabric and fold border over to the wrong side of fabric.

5 Turn under raw edges and hem in place by hand. Repeat this along all edges, mitring the three remaining corners. When completed, press.

BRAIDS

Braids are available in a wide range of colours and widths. Always select one suitable for the weight of fabric you are using. As a general rule with furnishings, keep to ornate braids for simple styles and use simple trims on fancy styles.

To attach, stitch along the centre of narrow braids and along both edges of wide braids. If the braid frays under the machine foot, attach it by hand using BACKSTITCH.

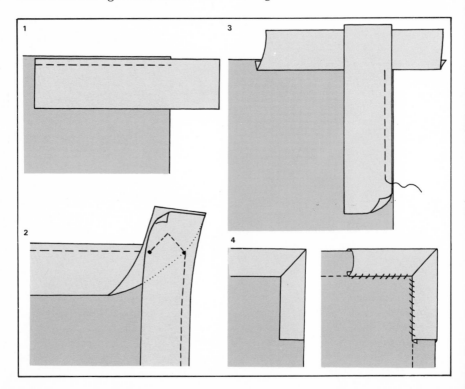

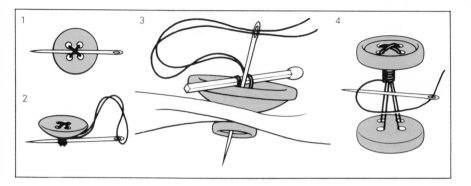

BUTTONS

Buttons should be carefully chosen for style and suitability. Too heavy a button will pull on the fabric. A fancy shape may look attractive but can tear the fabric. Take a fabric swatch with you to ensure a good match.

Buttons which are going through a buttonhole need a shank to allow for the thickness of the fabric between garment and button when it is done up.

To make a shank

1 Sew the button in the usual way but lay a cocktail stick or pin across the top of the button while you stitch through button and fabric.

2 Take thread down through button but not through fabric. Remove the stick or pin and wind thread firmly round threads under button. Take needle through to wrong side and fasten off.

Strong-back buttons

To prevent strain on heavy or loose-weave fabrics, a small flat button can be joined on the underside of the fabric.

3 Sew through both buttons, placing a match over the top button to make the shank.

Linked buttons

These can be used on bulky fabrics meeting edge to edge. Sew two or three strands of thread between two buttons.

4 Work BLANKET STITCH tightly over the threads and fasten off. The linked buttons are now ready to join cuffs or coat edges.

CANING

Chairs can easily be given a new look by simply recaning. Most commercial caning is available in sizes from 1 to 6 and for the traditional 6-step caning, you will need two sizes – 2 and 4. It is easier to work with damp cane which is more pliable, but do not soak the cane or it will become discoloured. Simply plunge into hot water.

You will also need pegs to hold the work tight (golf tees will work) and a clearer to clean out the holes before you start.

1 Start by placing size 2 cane in a hole next to one of the corners in the back rail. Leave 15cm (6in) underneath and peg cane tightly. Pass the cane

through the opposite hole in the front rail and peg it again. Now bring the cane up through the next hole in the front, making sure the glossy side is uppermost, and peg again. Take the cane to the back again and then forwards until all but the corner holes are used.

Leave the first peg in position as this holds the end of the cane secure. The second and third pegs are travelling pegs and move with your work. When a length of cane is nearing the end, peg into the next hole and start with a new

piece, pegged into position.

2 This is working horizontally in the same way as **1**. This stage of the caning lies on top of the vertical rows. Keep the glossy side of the cane up.

3 This is a repeat of the first vertical but lies on top of the first horizontal creating a 'sandwich' to hold the vertical strands of cane.

4 The second horizontal step follows the pattern of the first horizontal, but this time the cane is woven over and under the vertical steps. It is best not to pull the cane all the way through after each stroke. Thread through about six to eight verticals with only a few centimetres of free cane, and then pull it through. Do not be too concerned about the lines looking tidy at this stage; they can be neatened in steps 5 and 6.

5 Change to the size 4 cane. This step is worked in a series of right angles which will become a diagonal once the cane is tightened.

Secure the cane with a peg in the back left-hand corner hole. Weave down over the first pair of horizontals and then along and under the first pair

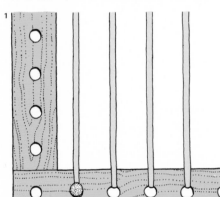

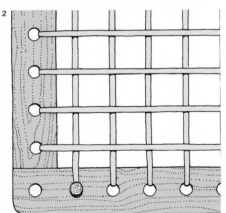

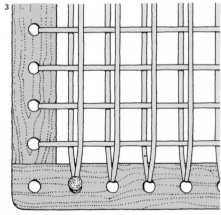

of verticals. Repeat this all the way across the seat until you reach the front rail. The first diagonal should finish in the opposite corner.

Bring the cane up through the next hole to the left in the front rail and weave back to the top of the left-hand rail. The pattern of the over and under weaving should be the same as the first line of diagonal weaving. Continue weaving back and forward until the front corner is reached and the cane is passed across the last two holes.

Return to the corner where this step began and peg another cane into that corner. Weave the other half of the seat in exactly the same way – over the horizontals and under the verticals.

6 This step requires working in the opposite direction of step **5**. Start in the back right-hand corner and weave at right angles to the other diagonal. This time you should weave under the horizontals and over the verticals. As for step **5**, make sure that the diagonals always slip between the horizontals and verticals.

Finishing off

To give a neat and tidy finish to the chair you need to peg or bead round the seat. This will hide the holes and put the finishing touch to the work.

7 Each hole may be pegged with pieces of no. 10 or 12 centre cane, cut to a shorter length than the depth of the rail. Insert one of these 'pegs' into each hole and tap them into place. Try to ensure that the pegs fit the hole tightly; if not use a thicker cane. Trim all surplus cane from the underside of the chair after pegging is complete to give a neat finish.

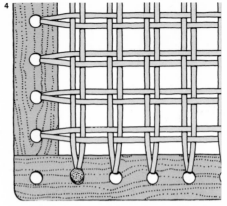

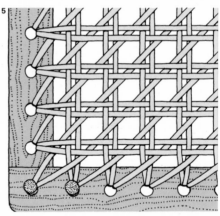

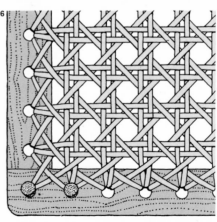

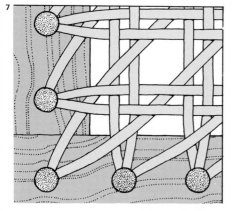

7

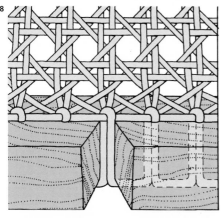

8

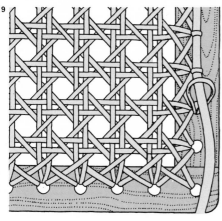

9

8 You may prefer the professional look of beading round the chair: take a length of no. 6 beading cane and trim one end to a point. Insert into a corner hole and bring the spare end beside the next hole on the left. Insert a no. 2 strand of cane down through this hole and secure under the frame.

9 Carry the other end over the beading cane and back through the same hole so that it forms a loop that traps the beading cane. Take the beading cane to the next hole on the left, bring the no. 2 cane up through it (as shown in cross section in **8**), loop over the beading cane and back again through the same hole. Always start a new piece at each corner hole.

Alternative uses

There are plenty of imaginative ways to use cane other than for chair seats. Its clean, airy appearance makes it ideal for a screen. This will let through a considerable amount of light, which makes it perfect as a room divider in a poorly lit room. The best way of covering the large area involved is to make several squares of identical caned frames and then set them in a timberwork frame and join the panels with hinges.

Cane may also be used for headboards, panelled doors and coffee tables which can then be covered with a glass top to protect the cane and ensure a flat surface.

Although cane is attractive in its natural state and will blend well with any colour scheme, it can be painted with acrylic paint. This paint is flexible when dry and will not peel off. Cane that has been painted black is ideal for a room with an oriental atmosphere.

COLOUR

Colour is a matter of personal choice, but when it comes to decorating and choosing furnishings there are a few basic guidelines that will help you create the effect you want.

The colour wheel below can be divided in half with the 'warm' colours on the left and the 'cool' colours on the right. Warm colours in a room tend to dominate and stand out, whereas cool colours tend to recede.

Study the room you are decorating – is it a small boxroom or a large, high-ceilinged room? Does it face north (cool) or south (warm)? To make a small room appear larger, go for the receding colours and plain or small print papers and fabrics. To make the most of a large room, use dominant colours and larger patterns.

Professionals often base their designs on the triadic colour harmony. This involves using any three colours that fall next to each other on the wheel.

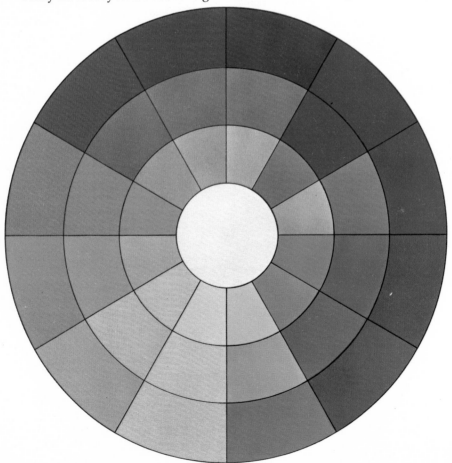

CORD

Cord can be used as a decorative trim on bedspreads, loose covers or, as shown here, to add a neat edge to embroidered CUSHIONS. Always check whether cord is pre-shrunk before buying and, if not, allow extra and wash before sewing. You can be adventurous in the colours you use.

Corded cushions

Pin cord around edge of finished cushion to cover the seam line. Make sure the ends of the cord meet along a side edge and not in a corner.

Leave 2.5cm (1in) free and then start sewing cord to cushion by passing matching thread through the cord and attaching it to the cushion with tiny stitches.

Sew all the way around but finish 2.5cm from where the cord will meet. To join the two ends, unravel the strands at both loose ends of the cord. Now cut 2.5cm off two strands of one unravelled end and the same from one strand of the other end. Twist the remaining ends together and stitch to cushion as before.

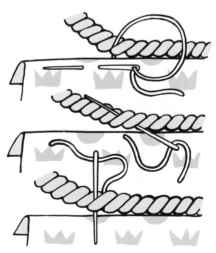

CROCHET

Crochet is simple to learn because it is based on just one stitch. Once you have learned these basic skills you can immediately move on to crochet your own clothes or furnishings.

Remember that crochet stitches are all variations of drawing one loop through another.

Chain stitch

1 Begin by making a slip loop on your hook with the end of the yarn. Hold the hook in your right hand, like you would a pencil.

2 Wind yarn round the little finger of the left hand. Take hook under the yarn so that you have a loop of yarn over the hook. This is described as yarn round hook. Draw the hook through the slip loop, taking the yarn caught round the hook with it. Pass the slip loop over the end of the hook. You now have one chain.

3 To make the next chain, take the yarn round the hook and draw the yarn through the loop on the hook. Pass the loop off the hook. Repeat until you have the required number to form your foundation chain.

Turning chains

Most crochet stitches are quite deep, so it is necessary to make a chain at the beginning of each row to bring your hook up to the right height before starting the next row. This does not apply, of course, when working circles or squares. The turning chain replaces the first stitch in the row, so it is important to remember to work into the top turning chain at the end of the next row, otherwise you will have lost a stitch.

Double crochet

Make 12 chain.

4 Insert hook into the third chain from

the hook, then take yarn round hook.

5 Draw yarn through so that there are two loops on the hook, yarn round hook again.

6 Draw yarn through both loops and slip them off hook. This makes one double crochet.

You will need to make two turning chain on a row of double crochet.

Treble crochet

Make 12 chain.

7 Yarn round hook, insert hook in the fourth chain from the hook, yarn round hook and draw yarn through (three loops on hook). Draw yarn round hook.

8 Draw yarn through first two loops (two loops on hook) then yarn round hook.

9 Draw yarn through both remaining loops. This makes one treble crochet.

You will need three turning chain on a row of treble crochet.

Slipstitch

This is a very shallow stitch and it is used mainly for shaping or for joining stitches when working in the round. Make 4 chain.

10 Insert hook into the next chain from the hook, from front to back, yarn round hook.

11 Draw yarn through both the chain and the loop on the hook.

Working in the round

Crochet is often worked in rounds instead of rows to give either a circular or square finished shape.

12 Make a length of chain and join the first chain with a slipstitch to make a circle. Stitches can then be worked into the centre of the circle rather than each individual chain.

Finishing off

After the last stitch, break off yarn about 10cm (4in) from the hook and

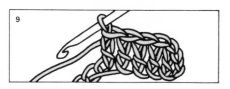

draw the end through the loop on the hook, pulling it tight to secure.

Yarns and hooks

There are many yarns suitable for crochet work. You can use knitting wools and cottons or for extra fine work there is a choice of mercerized crochet cottons. You might want to experiment, too, by working with string or ribbon or a combination to get an unusual effect.

Crochet hooks are available in many sizes to work with the different yarns. The larger hooks are made of aluminium or plastic, and the very fine hooks are made from steel.

Sizes range from the very thinnest 0.6mm (size 7) to 2mm (size 1½) which are used for fine cotton to make lace patterns. The large hooks, 2.5mm to 7mm (sizes 12 to 2), are used for the thicker yarns.

Hook sizes are recommended with all patterns, but always check your tension before starting any project.

Tension

There is much more variation in tension with crochet than there is with knitting. It is more likely, therefore, that you may have to change the size of the hook recommended in the pattern.

Work a sample square to a minimum of 10cm (4in) square with the suggested hook. If there are too many stitches, try a larger hook; if there are too few, try a smaller hook.

The crochet bedspread in this quaint attic-bedroom setting can be adapted to fit any sized bed. The squares in the pattern can be adapted to cushions and curtains.

CROCHET BEDSPREAD

The elegant bedspread shown on the previous pages is made up of squares with an added border. It is crocheted using a good quality dishcloth cotton. The squares can also be crocheted for curtains using the same border design (see graph below) to match the bed-cover. They can equally well be made up into cushions.

Abbreviations

beg	beginning
ch	chain
dc	double crochet
patt	pattern
rep	repeat
RS	right side
ss	slipstitch
sp	space
st(s)	stitch(es)
tr	treble
WS	wrong side
yrh	yarn round hook

Border design for crochet bedspread.

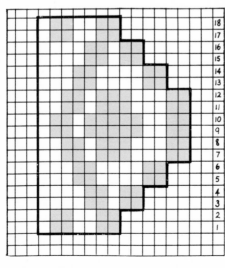

Materials

Single bed: 200cm by 250cm (6ft by 8ft) 29 100g hanks of cotton
Double bed: 250cm square (8ft square) 37 100g hanks of cotton
Queen size bed: 250cm by 300cm (8ft by 10ft) 45 100g hanks of cotton.
One 6mm (size 4) crochet hook

Squares

Work into the back loop only.
Make 6 ch, join into a ring with ss.
1st round 3 ch, 15 tr into the centre of the ring, ss to top of 3 ch.
2nd round *3 ch, miss one st, 1 dc in each of next 3 sts, rep from * 3 times more.
3rd round *3 ch, miss one st, 2 tr in next st, 1 tr in each of next 3 sts, 2 tr in next st, rep from * 3 times more.
4th round *3 ch, miss one st, 1 dc in each of next 9 sts, rep from * 3 times more.
5th round *3 ch, miss one st, 2 tr in next st, 1 tr in each of next 9 sts, 2 tr in next st, rep from * 3 times more.
6th round *3 ch, miss one st, 1 dc in each of next 15 sts, rep from * 3 times more.
7th round *3 ch, miss one st, 2 tr in next st, 1 tr in each of next 15 sts, 2 tr in next st, rep from * 3 times more.
8th round *3 ch, miss one st, 1 dc in each of next 2 sts, 3 ch, (yrh, insert hook in next st, yrh and draw through, yrh and draw through two loops on hook) twice, yrh and draw through two loops, yrh, insert hook in same st, yrh and draw through (yrh and draw through on two loops) 3 times – 1 bobble made – **1 dc in each of next 3 dc, 1 bobble in next st, rep from ** 3 times more, 1 dc in each of next 2 dc, rep from * 3 times more.
9th round *3 ch, miss one st, 2 tr in next st, 1 tr in each of next 21 sts, 2 tr in next

st, rep from * 3 times more.

10th round *3 ch, miss one st, 1 dc in each of next 27 sts, rep from * 3 times more.

11th round *3 ch, miss one st, 2 tr in next st, 1 tr in each of next 27 sts, 2 tr in next st, rep from * 3 times more.

12th round *3 ch, miss one st, 1 dc in each of next 33 sts, rep from * 3 times more.

13th round *3 ch, miss one st, (1 tr, 1 ch, 1 tr) all in next st, (1 ch, miss one st, 1 tr in next st) 16 times, 1 ch, miss one st, (1 tr, 1 ch, 1 tr) all in next st, rep from * 3 times more.

14th round *3 ch, miss one st, 1 dc in each of next 41 sts, rep from * 3 times more.

15th round *3 ch, miss one st, 2 tr in next st, 1 tr in each of next 41 sts, 2 tr in next st, rep from * 3 times more.

16th round *3 ch, miss one st, 1 dc in each of next 47 sts, rep from * 3 times more.

17th round *3 ch, miss one st, 2 tr in next st, 1 tr in each of next 47 sts, 2 tr in next st, rep from * 3 times more.

18th round *3 ch, miss one st, 1 dc in each of next 2 sts, 1 bobble in next st, (1 dc in each of next 3 sts, 1 bobble in next st) 12 times, 1 dc in each of next 2 sts, rep from * 3 times more.

19th round *3 ch, miss one st, 2 tr in next st, 1 tr in each of next 53 sts, 2 tr in next st, rep from * 3 times more.

20th round *3 ch, miss one st, 1 dc in each of next 59 sts, rep from * 3 times more.

21st round *3 ch, miss one st, 2 tr in next st, 1 tr in each of next 59 sts, 2 tr in next st, rep from * 3 times more, 2 ch, ss to top of first tr.

22nd round 4 ch, 1 tr in same st, 1 ch, 1 tr in next st, (1 ch, miss one st, 1 tr in next st) 30 times, 1 ch, miss one st, (1 tr, 1 ch, 1 tr) all in next st, *3 ch, miss one st, (1 tr, 1 ch, 1 tr) all in next st, (1 ch, miss one st, 1 tr in next st) 21 times, 1 ch, miss one st, (1 tr, 1 ch, 1 tr) in next st, rep from * twice more, 3 ch, ss to third of 4 ch.

Border Make 23 ch. Work in both loops of each st in the usual way throughout.
1st row 1 tr in 4th ch from hook, 1 tr in each of next 4 ch, 2 ch, miss 2 ch, 1 tr in next ch, 2 ch, miss 2 ch, 1 tr in each of next 7 ch, 2 ch, miss 2 ch, 1 tr in next ch, turn. 2nd row: 5 ch, 1 tr in each of next 7 tr, 2 ch, 1 tr in next tr, 2 ch, 1 tr in each of next 5 tr, 1 tr in top of 3 ch.

Continue working from chart (see far left), starting at row 1 again but thereafter only repeating rows 1 to 18.
Single bed: Work two lengths of 6 patt repeats each and two lengths of 8 patt repeats each.
Double bed: Work four lengths of 8 patt repeats each.
Queen size bed: Work two lengths of 8 patt repeats each and two lengths of 10 patt repeats each.

Always work the first two rows of the pattern repeat twice, at the beginning only of each length of border.

To complete
Single bed: Make 12 squares and join into 4 rows of 4 squares each.
Double bed: Make 16 squares and join into 4 rows of 4 squares each.
Queen size bed: Make 20 squares and join into 5 rows of 4 squares each.

Now either sew or crochet the squares together, right sides facing. Add the borders in the same way, finishing the ends of each border piece level with the outer edge of squares.

CURTAINS

A new pair of curtains can completely transform a room. Select the style carefully and choose a fabric which will complement your décor. Full-length curtains tend to look more formal than sill-length ones, which have more of a country look. Tie-back curtains can look very elegant made in velvet or brocade, and also look pretty and cheerful in a printed cotton. Sheers or café curtains are ideal where privacy is required and cross-over curtains add a feminine touch to a room.

Fabrics

For unlined curtains, lightweight fabrics which let the light filter through are the most suitable. Cotton, cotton mixtures, lightweight synthetics, sheers, nets and lace are all suitable. For lined curtains, medium to heavy-weight fabrics are more appropriate Choose chintz, furnishing cotton, velvet or brocade.

Weights

Weights help the curtains hang better and are available in two types: circular weights which are sewn into the

Cafe curtains in a kitchen keep out prying eyes and can be quickly and easily washed if they are accidentally splashed.

corners, or a tape of weights enclosed in the hem.

Headings

Different types of heading tape are now available, which makes it easy to produce exactly the style of curtain you want. The most common types are gathered, triple-pleated and pencil-pleated headings. Each of these headings requires a slightly different fullness: a standard gathered heading requires approximately 1½ times the width of the window, triple pleats twice the width and pencil pleats 2½ times the width.

Measuring up

To estimate the width of fabric required, measure the length of the

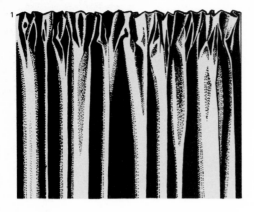

curtain pole. Multiply this measurement by the fullness required for the selected heading. Divide by two to get the required width for each curtain. Add 5cm (2in) for each side hem, plus 3cm (1¼in) for each join. Divide this measurement by the width of the chosen fabric to get the required number of drops (widths).

For the length, measure from the top of the track or bottom of the pole to the sill or floor. Add 15cm (6in) for the bottom hem, plus 4cm (1½in) for the top turning. Multiply this measurement by the number of drops required. This is the amount of fabric you need to buy. However, if the fabric has a large design, you need to buy an extra pattern repeat per drop, except for the first one. For example, if you need a total of four drops, buy three extra pattern repeats.

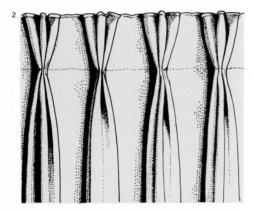

Above left: The required width of fabric for a gathered heading equals 1½ times to twice the length of the curtain pole.
Left: Triple-pleat curtains require a double fullness of fabric.
Below left: Pencil pleats require a fullness of 2¼ to 2½ times.

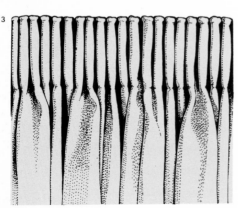

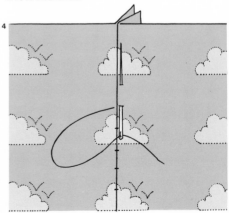

Making up

1 Before starting to cut out, ensure that you have a straight edge by pulling out a thread at the top of the fabric. Cut out all the drops, making sure that the pattern will run at exactly the same level on each one.

If your fabric has a pattern, fold under the seam allowance down the side of one drop and press. Lap the folded edge over the second drop and match up the pattern. Tack the two drops together. Turn the fabric over so that the right sides are facing and machine stitch along the tacking line. Turn under 1.5cm (½in) along each side and then another 3.5cm (1½in); press in place. Turn under a 7.5cm (3in) wide double hem along the bottom. MITRE the corners, HERRING-BONE stitch the hems in place and SLIPSTITCH the mitres to close.

2 Measure off the finished length of each curtain and turn the surplus fabric to the wrong side along the top. Cut off a length of heading tape, turn under the raw ends and pin and tack in place, covering the raw edge of the fabric. Pull out the cords at both ends and knot them together at one end. The latter side should be positioned at the centre of the window, so make a left and a right curtain. Stitch by machine all round, close to the edge, taking care not to stitch over the loose cords.

3 Gently pull up the gathers until the curtains measure the correct width, spacing the gathers evenly. Knot the ends together.

4 Insert curtain hooks fairly close together and mount the curtains on the track.

For lined curtains, see Linings.

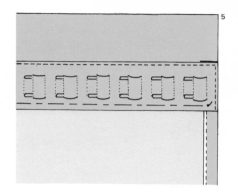

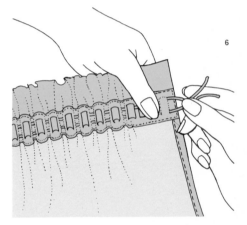

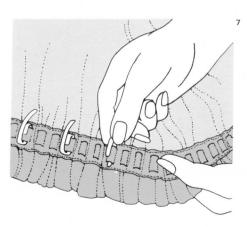

CUSHIONS

Cushions are both functional and decorative and require only a minimum of fabric. They can be used on chair seats for extra comfort or scattered on beds and sofas to add interest to a room. The size and shape can be varied to suit individual requirements; round, square and rectangular cushion pads are available in department stores in several sizes. However, if you want a more unusual shape, simply make a pad in the same way as the outer cover, omitting any trimmings. Use ticking for the cover and feathers for the filling.

Styles can be varied endlessly. Almost any material can be used, and techniques such as APPLIQUÉ, PATCHWORK, QUILTING and EMBROIDERY lend themselves beautifully to the decoration of cushions. Leftover fabrics from other soft furnishing projects come in handy, and old dresses and blouses can be put to practical use again, for example in a patchwork cushion. Tray cloths, perhaps with lace edging, or fringed scarves can be made into individual and beautiful cushion covers, and lace and broderie Anglaise look delightful either as entire covers or as frills inserted in the side seams.

Piping provides a smart, tailored finish to cushions and is particularly suitable for an elegant décor. For a cheerful and informal room, a frilled edge may be more appropriate.

Left: A wide range of mix-and match fabrics and co-ordinating wallpapers are available today to make home decorating exciting and yet simple. Use leftover fabrics from, for example, loose covers to make a pile of attractive scatter cushions.

35

Making a square cover

Using dressmaker's graph paper, mark a square the required size of the finished cushion. Add 1.5cm (½in) all round for seam allowances. You will need twice this amount of fabric for one cushion.

1 Cut out the fabric pieces. If you want to pipe the cushion cover, make up a length of piping equal to the circumference of the cushion, plus a few centimetres for joining ends (see instructions on page 89). Starting at the centre of one side and matching raw edges, place the piping on the right side of one fabric piece. Tack in place as close to the piping cord as possible, leaving 5cm (2in) unstitched on each side of the join. Unpick the piping and join the bias strips along the straight grain as usual. Cut off the cords so that the ends butt together and bind them with sewing thread. Fold the fabric back over the cord and tack the rest of the piping in place. Stitch by machine using a zipper foot. Clip into the corners of the piping fabric.

2 With right sides together and raw edges matching, place the second fabric piece on the first. Pin, tack and machine stitch, using the previous stitching line as a guide. Leave a fairly wide opening along one side. Trim seam allowances and cut diagonally across the corners. Turn the cover right side out, insert cushion pad and slipstitch the opening to close.

Box cushions

Estimate the amount of fabric required for the main pieces in the same way as for a square cushion. For the gusset, measure the length and depth of each side and add 1.5cm (½in) all round for seam allowances. You will also need a zip the length of the back of the cushion plus one side.

3 Cut out all fabric pieces. With right sides together and raw edges matching, pin, tack and stitch the short edges of the gusset strips together to make a ring. Press seams open. With right sides together and seams and corners matching, place the gusset around the top fabric piece. Pin, tack and stitch.

4 On the bottom piece, along the back and halfway down each adjoining

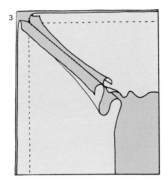

side, press the seam allowances to the wrong side. Clip with the scissors into the allowances at the ends of the fold line and at the corners. With the face down and teeth over the fold line, pin, tack and stitch the zip to the wrong side of the bottom piece. With right sides together and raw edges matching, pin, tack and stitch the rest of the bottom piece and the other side of the zip to the gusset. Open the zip partly before tacking. Clip corners and turn the cover right side out.

Circles and hexagons
5 Make a square paper pattern, each side of which is equal to the required diameter, including a 1.5cm (½in) seam allowance all round. Fold the pattern in half and then in half again. Using a pencil on a string, secured with a drawing pin at corner A, draw an arc from B to C. Cut out the pattern.
6 For a hexagon, use the circular template and mark off the radius of the circle six times round the circle and join up the points. Cut out the pattern.

Round and hexagonal cushions alike require two pieces of fabric the same size as the pattern. Make them in the same way as square cushions on page 36.

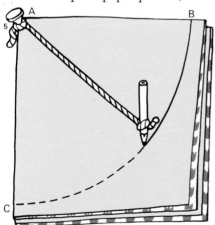

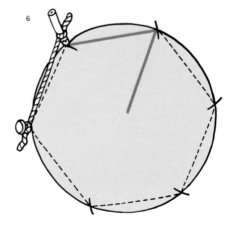

Right: Mix fabrics and patterns to great effect by making a group of patchwork cushions for a sofa or a window seat. Use the same range of fabrics, but design each cushion individually for a striking result.

Below: Round cushions can add great charm to a room. They look particularly pretty with a scalloped edge.

DÉCOUPAGE

The art of découpage – cutouts – first started in Italy when artisans, unable to master the intricate handpainting of the Chinese, tried to imitate the effect by gluing cutouts to furniture.

Découpage is now a popular craft in which motifs are used to decorate a wooden or painted background. Clear varnish is then applied until the picture is buried beneath anything up to 30 coats. The picture will then glow through the layer of varnish as if it is painted on to the original woodwork. This technique can be successfully used to decorate screens, boxes, furniture (see illustration overleaf), bedheads, or any plain flat surface.

Choice of motifs

The best cutouts for découpage are on thin paper as these will need fewer coats of varnish to cover the edges. Look through old wallpaper pattern books, cut out sections of gift wrapping paper, use old photos or even colourful postage stamps. Remember, though, once sealed, whatever you use is there to stay.

However tempting, avoid using cutouts from books and magazines as you will find you have a see-through problem with the print from the other side of the page.

Cutting out

There is a trick to cutting out the more delicate shapes. First, use a good pair of nail scissors with curved blades. Alternatively, any sharp scissors about 7.5cm (3in) long will do. Now, holding the paper in your left (or non-working) hand, place the scissors where you intend to start cutting and

move the paper smoothly through the blades. The hand holding the scissors should not move.

Arrange the cutouts on your background until you are satisfied with the layout. If necessary, pencil in their positions. Spread adhesive (wallpaper paste is ideal because it does not stain) evenly over the back of your cutout. Place in position and press firmly – you can use a wallpaper roller for a smooth finish and to remove any air bubbles under the paper. If large bubbles persist, you can make a small slit in the print and press the air and adhesive out. The slit will not show up later. Leave to dry.

Varnishing

Spray the pasted-down picture with artist's fixative. Leave to dry and then wipe with a lintless cloth – do not use tissues or cotton wool as they will leave fibres on your work. Dip just the end of your brush into the polyurethane varnish and apply the first coat. Always use long strokes and lift the brush clear at the end of each stroke. Leave the work to dry thoroughly in a dust-free place.

Modern polyurethane gloss varnishes dry very quickly. However some may have a yellowish tinge to them which will make a white background look rather yellow when the work is finished. Clear no-colour varnish, specially for découpage work, can be bought at most good craft supply shops.

Try to keep your work in as dust-free an environment as possible. If you are decorating a small box, place it in a larger box to dry. A piece of furniture can be covered with a tent made of polythene sheeting. Apply about ten coats of varnish, allowing each to dry thoroughly. By this stage, the edges of the cutout should have been covered and you will not be able to feel them through the varnish.

Sanding down

Wrap a piece of very fine sandpaper, or flour paper, round a matchbox and rub over the varnished surface using a circular motion. Wash the surface clean and wipe dry. Rub down with steel wool. Rub clean again and you are ready for the next coat of varnish. From now on, rub down between coats of varnish. The advantage of rubbing down is that it will give a better surface for the next coat of varnish to adhere to.

When about 30 coats have been applied, give a final polish with a good wax polish.

DUVET COVERS

A duvet is an increasingly popular form of bedding that replaces the conventional top sheet and blankets. They are light to sleep under, retain the heat well and take all the headache out of making beds.

Duvets are available with a number of different fillings. You can choose from goose or duck down, feathers, or a mixture of feathers and down. The synthetic fillings, such as polyester, are popular as they can be laundered and are suitable for people with allergies. Of all the fillings available, pure down is the warmest, but all will provide a warm covering.

The warmth of a duvet is now measured by its tog rating – an internationally recognized unit. The minimum rating for a duvet is 7.5 togs and the higher the number, the warmer your quilt will be. You may prefer to have two single duvets on a double bed, especially if one person is a restless sleeper or prefers a different degree of warmth.

Cutting out

For a *single* duvet cover, cut two rectangles of fabric 150cm × 213cm (59in × 83in). For a *double* duvet cover, cut two rectangles of fabric 213cm × 213cm (83in × 83in).

1

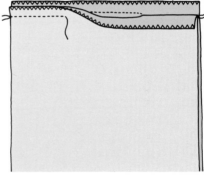

2

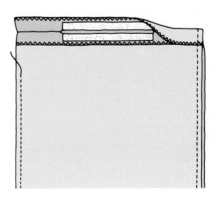

Making the cover

First prepare the bottom end of the cover to take the Velcro fastening, by neatening the two raw edges with ZIGZAG stitch. Turn back a hem of 2.5cm (1in) to the wrong side. Press.

1 With right sides of the fabric together, stitch the two bottom edges of the cover together along the crease line, leaving an opening in the centre

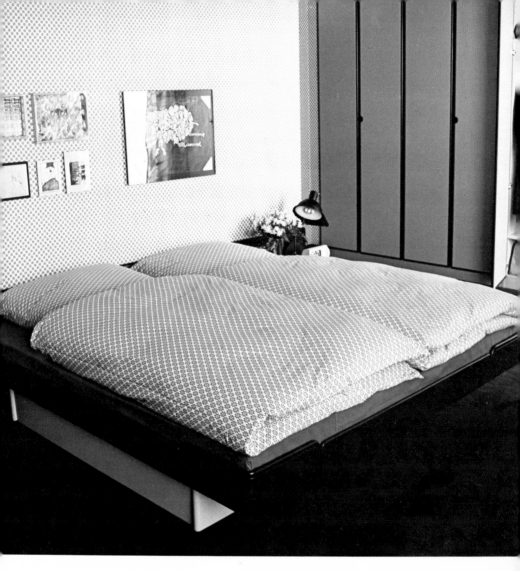

large enough to insert the duvet later. Cut the Velcro strips to length.

2 Stitch the Velcro to each side of the opening. Press the turnings in.

With right sides facing, machine the remaining three sides together, taking 1.5cm (½in) turnings at the corners and neatening them with a zigzag stitch. Turn the cover through to the right side and press.

Above: A clever idea for partners who require different degrees of warmth at night. Matching covers hold duvets with different fillings.

Left: A folksy way to brighten up an old chest. Cut-out flowers are buried beneath coats of varnish for the découpage effect of handpainted wood.

DYEING

To give clothes or household linen a new lease of life, try a change of colour. Most fabrics, including some synthetics, can be dyed at home, but do check manufacturer's labels for fibre content and washing advice. If a fabric is washable it is generally true that it can also be dyed. This does not apply, however, to acrylics, such as Orlon, Courtelle and Acrilan, and to fabrics with dripdry or non-iron finishes.

Two kinds of dye can be bought to use at home: hot or cold water dyes.

Hot water dyes
These are available in liquid or powder form and may be used on all natural fabrics and a wide range of synthetics.

Cold water dyes
These dyes come only in powder form and are used in conjunction with a fixing agent. They are best used on natural fabrics, although you can dye fabric mixtures that have a high proportion of cotton. As only the cotton will pick up the dye, remember that the shade will end up paler than shown on the pack.

Both types of dye may be used for either hand or machine dyeing. There is also a special washing machine pack on the market which combines a hot water dye with a low-suds detergent to wash and dye at the same time.

Choosing a colour
If you want to dye an article that is white or cream, you should get a match close to that on the dye pack. However, if you are dyeing a coloured item, refer to the above chart for the new colour.

Dyeing guide

Base colour		Dye Colour		Result
Brown	+	Red	=	Rust
Blue	+	Yellow	=	Green
Green	+	Red	=	Brown
Green	+	Yellow	=	Lime
Pink	+	Light blue	=	Lilac
Red	+	Blue	=	Purple
Red	+	Yellow	=	Orange
Yellow	+	Pink	=	Coral
Yellow	+	Purple	=	Brown

Follow instructions
All brands of dye come with full instructions which should be followed.

Make sure your dye container is roomy enough for the article to move about freely. If it is squashed into too small a container you will get an uneven finish. The bath, sink or plastic bowl can be used for cold water dyes. Use a flameproof container for dyeing small articles with hot water. Use the washing machine for larger items or to colour match small ones.

French dyeing
You can get an interesting effect by dyeing only the edge of an item.

Mix up the dye as per the instructions. Wet the article to be dyed thoroughly and gradually immerse one end of it into a bowl of dye. You will have to rig up a hanger to let the item hang in the bowl for the required length of time. You can get two or more shades of the same colour by leaving a section of the border in the dye for longer.

EMBROIDERY STITCHES

Embroidery adds an individual charm to household linens as well as clothes. With just a few basic stitches you can tackle most embroidery projects or design your own to add a personal touch.

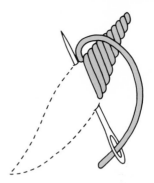

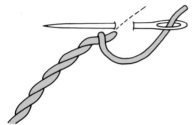

Stem stitch

Stem stitch is good for working curved outlines or for flower stems. It gives a thicker outline than backstitch as the stitches overlap each other. With short stitches you will get a well-defined ridge; long stitches produce a finer, feathery look.

Bring the needle up on the right side of the material. Take a stitch to the right then bring the needle up halfway back along the stitch line. Make the next stitch in the same way.

Satin stitch

Satin stitch is probably one of the most popular flat stitches and is used to work a block of embroidery in one colour. For a raised effect, first pad the area with running stitches.

Make each stitch by inserting the needle on one side of the design and bringing it up through the fabric on the other side. Pull the thread gently until the stitch lies flat on the fabric. Try to keep all the stitches parallel as you work.

Satin stitch is ideal for small designs on linens or clothing and can be used effectively to fill in petals or for working monograms on handkerchiefs or dressing-gowns, for example.

Chain stitch

Chains form a neat, slightly raised effect. Use them to outline shapes worked in satin stitch or for a decorative edge around motifs in APPLIQUÉ work.

Bring the thread through from the back of the fabric. Hold a loop of thread down with your thumb and insert the needle where it first came through, bringing out the needle slightly further along. Work each stitch similarly so that it holds the previous stitch in place and gradually forms a chain.

45

FASTENERS

There are a variety of fastenings to choose from, but for a professional finish to your work, each should be applied in the correct way.

Press studs (1)

A press stud has less holding power than a hook and eye and is used on overlapping edges where the fastener should not show. The ball part goes on the underside of the overlap and is sewn on first. Close the overlap and mark with chalk where the socket part should lie. Sew in position.

Hooks and eyes (2)

These are available in a wide range of sizes – small ones are best for fine fabrics, larger ones for heavy fabrics. To attach, embroider tiny blanket stitches over the hook and eye so that the metal is covered. A thread loop, also made with blanket stitches over a double loop, can be worked to replace the metal eye.

Hook and eye tape (3)

Useful where there is a need for several hooks and eyes and where the tape would make the fastening more comfortable to wear if against the skin. The tape can be machine stitched or hand-sewn in position. Sew the hook side on first and carefully mark the exact place for the eyes as any incorrect alignment will throw the whole row out.

Velcro (4)

The easiest fastener to apply, Velcro is made from two nylon strips with surfaces that cling to each other until pulled apart. The tape can be machine or hand stitched all the way around.

FELT

Felt is an excellent fabric to work with because it is easy to cut and does not fray. This makes it particularly suitable for beginners experimenting with APPLIQUÉ work. It can also be glued into position using a standard fabric glue, such as Copydex. Felt is available in an impressive range of colours, lengths and squares, which also makes it ideal for simple patchwork. It can be used for soft toys, belts and rugs, as well as a wide range of household items. The only disadvantage of working with felt is that it is not washable, but it dry cleans well.

Do not iron felt backwards and forwards in the usual way as this will stretch it. Press under a damp cloth with a warm iron. Direct heat will leave a shiny mark.

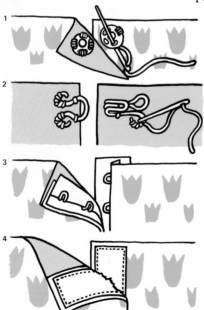

FESTOON BLINDS

The soft folds of a festoon blind make it particularly suitable for a bedroom. These blinds are similar to ROMAN BLINDS, except that they have cords which draw the fabric up into soft horizontal folds.

Buying the fabric

The best kinds of fabric are those which are fine and will gather gently. Cotton lawns, seersucker, silks or synthetic silks are all ideal. Avoid large geometric patterns which will look wrong once ruched into the folds of a festoon.

Elegant festoon blinds.

First decide whether you want your blind to hang inside or outside the window recess. For an inside blind, measure the width and height inside the recess. For an outside blind, take the measurements outside the recess and add 5cm (2in) on each side of the width. You will need to buy approximately twice the width in fabric, plus an extra 20cm (8in) for the length. If you plan to add a frill along the bottom, allow extra for this. You may prefer to use BIAS BINDING or a decorative FRINGE.

47

Making the blind

Cut the fabric into the required lengths and, if necessary, make any joins using a FRENCH SEAM. Sew a double hem 1.5cm (½in) wide on the side edges.

Place the fabric on a flat work surface, wrong side up. Mark the position for vertical rows of cotton tape with pins. Place the first lengths of tape at each side edge over the double hem and the remaining tapes at equal intervals of between 30 and 35cm (12 and 14in) across the width of the blind. Pin and stitch tapes to blind.

Now turn under a 1.5cm (½in) hem along the top edge of the blind and press. Place a length of curtain heading tape across the top of the blind so that it covers the raw edge of the fabric and the tapes. Knot the cords at one end and then machine the tape in place.

Frills or fringe

If you are making a frill for the blind, cut a length of fabric twice the width of the blind. Make a double hem all around and stitch. Run a row of gathering stitches about 1.5cm (½in) down from the top of the frill, and another one 5mm (¼in) below. Pull to gather until the frill matches blind width and machine in place on the blind. The fringe should be cut to the width of the blind and sewn along the bottom edge.

Threading the cord

Stitch curtain rings, at equal distances of 25cm (10in) down each tape, starting the rings 15cm (6in) down from the top (shown above). Make sure that all the rings align horizontally.

Take a length of wooden batten, the exact width of the blind, and attach it to the wall. Fix a length of curtain track to the front of the batten.

Pull the gathering cord in the curtain heading until the blind is the width of the curtain track. Slide curtain hooks into the heading tape. Screw the picture rings into the base of the batten so that each hook corresponds with each vertical tape.

Cut lengths of cord for each vertical tape. Every length of cord should be 2½ times the length of the tape. Tie one end of the first length of cord securely to the bottom left-hand ring and thread the cord up through all the rings on the left-hand tape.

Thread the blind on to the curtain track, remembering to slot the hooks at each end of the heading into the end stops to keep it safe. Thread the left-hand cord through the row of picture rings in the batten and out through the last ring on the right. Do the same with all the other cords until they hang free on the right-hand side.

Attach a cleat on to the wall by the right side of the blind. Cut off the lengths of cord so that they hang level with the bottom of the blind and knot them together. The blind can now be raised and lowered with the cords.

FILLINGS

Soft toys, sag bags and cushions can be filled with a variety of materials.

Foam chips are economical and good for large toys and sag bags, but may give a lumpy finish unless cased inside a thick fabric.

Kapok comes from a cotton plant and is very light and easy to use. It makes a good soft filling for a child's toy. It may go lumpy and hard if washed, though.

Filling made from *synthetic fibre* is sold tightly packed and should be teased out before use. It has the advantage of being washable.

If you use *clean rags and old tights* or stockings, cut them up into small pieces first. These are also washable.

Beware: All commercial fillings are flammable.

FLAT FELL SEAMS

These are used to join medium to heavyweight fabrics where a completely enclosed seam is desirable.

1 With the wrong sides of the fabric together, pin, tack and stitch a 2.5cm (1in) wide seam. Trim one of the seam allowances to 1cm (½ in) from the machine stitches. Press the seam towards the narrower edge.

2 Fold the wide seam allowance over the trimmed edge and pin. Tack, and machine close to the edge.

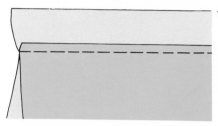

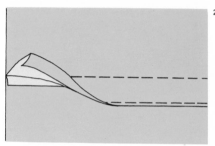

FRENCH SEAMS

These are used for joining widths of fabric where a strong, neat join is required on lightweight fabrics and

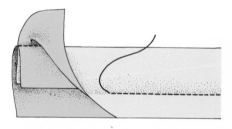

where the seam could fray. Tack along the seam line on each of the pieces of fabric. Place the pieces, wrong sides together, and stitch along the length of the seam, halfway between the seam line and the raw edges of the fabric. Press open the seam. Fold back the fabric, right sides together and sew along tacking line, enclosing the first seam and both raw edges.

49

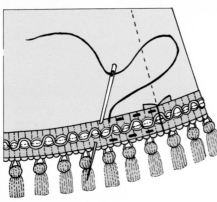

FRINGES

Fringes are usually used to add a decorative edge to LAMPSHADES. They can also give a glamorous look along the edge of a BLIND, round the hem of a bedspread, or a silky fringe can be sewn round a circular tablecloth. If you are using a fringe on TABLE LINEN check whether it is washable or will need dry cleaning.

If you are using a fringe as a trim for a lampshade, it should be stitched by hand, except in the case of a hard lampshade when it is best applied with a recommended fabric adhesive, such as Copydex.

Stitch the trimming with small stitches, making sure that they will not show on the inside of the shade. To join the two ends, turn in the fringe approx 1.5cm (½in) and butt the ends together.

50

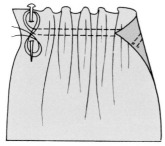

GATHERING

Gathering is a decorative way to achieve fullness; soft fabrics create the most attractive gathers and you should allow 1½ times the final gathered length when estimating fabric.

By hand

Fasten the thread at the beginning of the row with several BACKSTITCHES. Work two rows of RUNNING STITCHES, one under the other. Pull up the needle end of the thread to make gathers.

By machine

Machine gathering is quicker to work, but the effect is not as soft. Work two rows, using a long stitch, one on the seam line and the other 5mm (¼in) from it. Leave long threads at both ends, anchoring one end by winding round a pin. Draw up the threads from the other end.

HEMMING

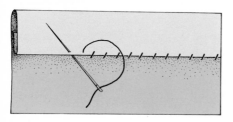

Hemming is a delicate stitch which can be used over a hem edge so that the stitches will not be visible on the right side of the work.

Work from right to left or towards you, holding the edge you are stitching over the index finger of your other hand. Take a tiny stitch in the article and then insert the needle point diagonally under the hem edge about 5mm (¼in) away. Pull thread through and repeat. If you cannot find an exactly matched thread, choose one a shade darker.

HERRINGBONE STITCH

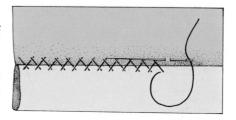

Herringbone is a particularly useful stitch for hemming when only a single turn is required, as it protects the raw edge. It is suitable for hemming curtains as the thread is not pulled tight and it makes a good loose hem. It can also be used for hemming skirts.

Herringbone is worked from left to right: bring the needle through from the back above the hem edge and make a stitch diagonally across into the hem. Now make a small stitch backwards, parallel with the hem line. Bring the needle through and across diagonally again to the top. Make another small stitch backwards and then repeat, as before. Try to keep the stitches equidistant and fairly loose as you work.

INTERLINING

Modern interlining fabrics are not as thick as wadding but are washable and will add thickness to machine quilting. They are most often used when making curtains placed between the fabric and lining material. The interlining provides extra insulation as well as plumping out the fabric which makes it drape better and shows it off to its best advantage.

Interlining fabrics are thick and fluffy but the additional weight may mean you need extra strong curtain rods or tracks.

The usual fabrics for interlining are bump and domette. Bump is the thicker of the two and is rather like a flannelette sheet. It is available in beige or white and is used to interline the heavier fabrics, such as velvet or brocade, which are used in traditional drapes. Domette is a similar material but lighter and less fluffy. This is the more usual interlining for lighter fabrics, such as cotton. Both types of interlining are available in the furnishing width of 122cm (48in).

Interlining curtains

To estimate the amount of fabric you will need measure as for curtains (see page 30), less the heading and turning allowance. Join the lengths of interlining together to make up the necessary width by overlapping the edges by 1.5cm (½in), placing the wrong side of one width over the right side of the other. Set the machine to a large stitch and join lengths with two rows of straight machine stitching.

Now lay the curtain out flat with the wrong side up. Place the interlining over the curtain so that it is positioned 20cm (8in) down from the top edge and 20cm (8in) up from the bottom edge. Fold back the interlining lengthways and join to the curtain fabric using LOCK STITCH (see page 69). Each row of lock stitches should be about 35cm (14in) apart.

Trim the sides so the interlining is 5cm (2in) in from the sides of the curtain and then HERRINGBONE STITCH the interlining to the curtain. Finally turn in 5cm (2in) of the curtain fabric to the wrong side down each side edge and herringbone in place. Make a double hem at the bottom of the curtain, mitring the corners (see page 74), and then hand hem. Don't cut off any fabric in case you need to let the curtains down later.

KNIFE PLEATS

This is a neat and elegant way to finish off the loose covers (see page 73) on chairs or sofas. Knife pleats require a strip of fabric three times the total measurement round the base of the sofa or chair.

Start by folding the strip of fabric in half and marking the centre. Cut a cardboard marker to the required width of your pleat and work halfway round the strip, pinning the pleats in place. When you reach the marked centre point, reverse the direction of the pleats so that you create one inverted centre pleat. This will give a professional look to the finished cover.

Try to work it so that a gap between pleats falls at each front corner. Test pin border to the cover, check hem depth and make any necessary adjustments. Hem by hand or machine before stitching the pleated strip to the cover.

KNITTING

Knitting is an easy and relaxing craft and a creative and economic way of making clothes for friends and family. Once you have got the hang of the basic stitches, you will be able to follow most patterns, or make the colourful liquorice allsorts shown on page 55.

Materials

Knitting needles are available in a wide range of shapes and sizes. For most projects, though, you will only need one pair of needles. The size of needle will depend on the type of yarn and the appearance of the garment.

Yarn can be bought in assorted thicknesses and textures, which may at first seem confusing. The thickness of wool is described as the 'ply', and the lower the number of the ply, the finer the yarn. A 2-ply yarn, for example, will have two strands twisted together as one; 3-ply yarn will have three strands and 4-ply will have four. After that, there is double-knitting, triple-knitting, double-double knitting and thicker-knit.

Basic stitches

It is best to learn the stitches by using thick wool and large needles.

Casting on

1 Make a slip loop near the end of the yarn and pull it firmly, but not too tightly, around the end of one needle, held in the left hand.

2 Hold the long end of the wool with the right hand and wind wool around the fingers, as shown. This may feel awkward at first, but with practice will feel more comfortable and will allow you to control the tension of the wool.

3 Keep the yarn to the back of the right-hand needle and, using the right hand, insert the right needle into the slip loop below the left-hand needle. Wind the wool under and over the right needle.

4 Pull the new loop through the first loop.

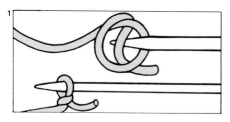

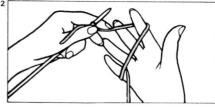

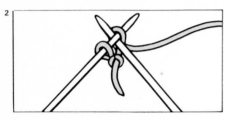

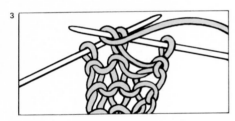

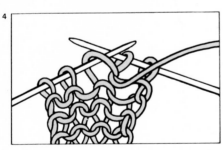

5 Place the new loop on the left-hand needle, pulling it close round the needle so that it matches the first loop.
6 Insert the needle between the first and second loop, wind the wool over and under again to make the third loop.

Continue until you have made the required number of stitches.

Knit stitch

Hold the needle with the stitches in the left hand. Place the point of the right needle through the front of the first stitch, holding the wool as described in casting on. Wind the wool under and over, as for casting on. Pull the new loop through the first loop, but keep it on the right-hand needle and slip the end stitch off the left-hand needle.

Place the right needle into the next stitch and repeat. Continue in this way until you reach the end of the row, when all the stitches will be on the right needle. Turn the work around and hold in the left hand and repeat the pattern.

When every stitch on every row is worked this way it is called garter stitch.

Purl stitch

This stitch is combined with knit stitch to make stocking stitch. It is produced by alternating one row of knit stitch with one row of purl stitch. This is the most common form of knitting seen on clothing.
7 Hold the needles as before, but with the wool at the front. Insert the right needle from right to left into the front of the stitch. Wind the wool over and under the right needle.
8 Pull the new loop through the old one which is then slipped off the left-hand needle.

Decreasing

The easiest way to decrease is to knit two stitches together. This can be done

The right side of stocking stitch (above) is smooth and is made by knitting one row plain and one row purl throughout.

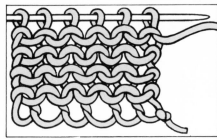

The other side is more textured and is called reversed stocking stitch.

either into the front or back of the stitches. Alternatively, two stitches can be purled together if you are working on a purl row.

Increasing

The most popular way to increase the number of stitches is to knit or purl into a stitch twice. On a knit stitch, knit as usual without slipping stitch off the needle, then knit into the back of the same stitch, keeping the yarn at the back of the work.

On a purl stitch, purl in the normal way but, again, do not slip stitch off the needle. Purl into the back of the same stitch, keeping the yarn at the front of the work.

Casting off

Knit the first two stitches, then insert the left needle into the first of these stitches and lift it over the second stitch and off the end of the right needle.

Knit the third stitch and then pass the second stitch over and off the third stitch. Continue in this way until you get to the last stitch. Break off the yarn, pull it through the loop and knot.

Intarsia

This is a method of knitting with two or more colours in any one row without taking the yarns across the back of the work. If a colour is used more than once in the row, separate balls of yarn are used and the back will be almost identical to the front.

Intarsia is usually knitted from a graph. This is simply because each square represents one stitch. Read from the bottom row upwards from right to left when the right side of the work is facing you. Change stitch, colour or yarn, as indicated on the graph.

At the join between two colours, twist the two around each other firmly at the back of the work to link the sections before finishing the row.

Abbreviations

dec	decrease
g st	garter stitch
inc	increase
K	knit
P	purl
psso	pass slipped stitch over
rep	repeat
RS	right side

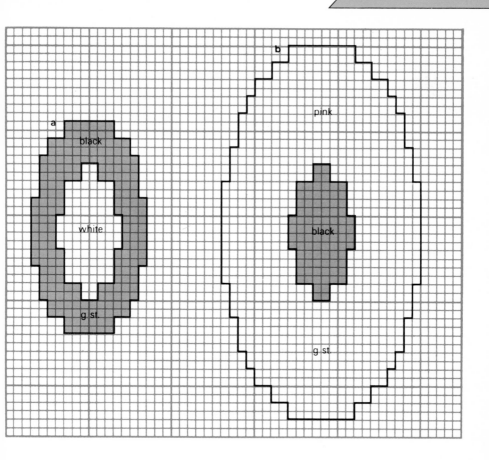

sl	slip
st(s)	stitch(es)
st st	stocking stitch
tog	together
WS	wrong side
wyif	with yarn in front
wyib	with yarn in back
yrn	yarn round needle

LIQUORICE ALLSORTS

This colourful beginner's project is worked in garter stitch using thick wool, and large, easy to handle needles.

Materials

One pair 7mm (No. 2) needles
Large bag of crumbled foam for filling.
Alternatively use solid foam cubes.
Use thick knit yarn.

Black and orange cube
100g (3½oz) black
50g (2oz) orange
Yellow and black cube
200g (7oz) yellow
50g (2oz) black
Black and white allsort
100g (3½oz) black

57

50g (2oz) white
Round black and white allsort
100g (3½oz) black
50g (2oz) white
Round pink and black allsort
200g (7oz) pink
50g (2oz) black

Instructions

Black and orange cube
Side pieces (knit 4):
Using black, cast on 22 sts. Work in garter stitch. K 8 rows black, 8 rows orange, 8 rows black and 8 rows orange. Cast off.
End pieces:
Using black, cast on 22 sts. K 40 rows. Cast off.
Sew up the cube leaving one seam open. Fill with crumbled foam and sew up the remaining seam.
Yellow and black cube
Side pieces (knit 4):
Using yellow, cast on 22 sts. K 16 rows yellow, 8 rows black and 16 rows yellow. Cast off.
End pieces (knit 2):
Using yellow, cast on 22 sts. K 40 rows. Cast off.
Finish off as for black and orange cube.
Black and white allsort
Side pieces (knit 4):
Using black, cast on 22 sts. K 8 rows black, 8 rows white and 8 rows black. Cast off.
End pieces (knit 2):
Using black, cast on 22 sts. K 40 rows. Cast off.
Sew up as for black and orange cube.
Round black and white allsort
Side piece (knit 1):
Using black, cast on 22 sts. K 80 rows. Leave sts on a holder with a length of yarn long enough for sewing up.

End pieces (knit 2):
These round end pieces have a white circle in the middle of the black. Its position is shown in the graph on page 57. Each square represents one stitch. Use two separate balls of black and one of white, twisting the ends of the two colours where they meet. The back will look like a series of white running stitches around the inner edge of the black circle.

To finish, neaten the four ends of yarn on the back of the intarsia circles. Sew up the cylinder. Sew in one end and half of the second. Fill with crumbled foam and sew up opening.
Round pink and black allsort
Side piece (knit 1):
Using pink, cast on 22 sts. K 140 rows. Leave sts on holder with a length of yarn for sewing up.
End pieces (knit 2):
Follow the graph, using the intarsia method. Sew up as described above.

Knitting care

Hours of hand knitting can easily be ruined unless you take care to follow washing instructions. Yarn wrappers now carry international symbols which advise on washing, ironing, dry cleaning and bleaching of that particular yarn.

LACE

Old lace – in the form of tablecloths, runners, collars and handkerchiefs – is becoming increasingly popular and beautiful displays can now be seen at weekend markets, jumble sales and antique shops.

Always hand wash old lace in a mild soapy solution. Pull gently into shape and dry flat. Iron on top of a towel so

that the surface of the lace will not be pressed completely flat.

Lacy cushion

To make one of the pretty cushions shown here you will need four lace-edged handkerchiefs and a square of fine cotton fabric for the cushion back.

Using ZIGZAG STITCH on the sewing machine, join the handkerchiefs together through the lace edges to make a square. If you are sewing by hand, use tiny oversewing stitches to join the handkerchiefs.

Cut the cotton backing fabric to the same size as the joined handkerchiefs. Turn a hem on all four sides so that the square fits the fabric area of the seamed handkerchiefs, leaving the lace edges free.

Machine stitch right on the edge, leaving one side open. Insert the cushion pad and close the remaining seam with tiny slip stitches.

Make a decorative trim in narrow satin, in white or a contrasting colour, and sew it to the middle of the cushion to finish.

59

LAMPSHADES

Lampshade-making is a rewarding craft and a real money-saver. It gives you the opportunity to produce a lampshade which is ideally suited to your own home. For example, make one in the same fabric as your CURTAINS or LOOSE COVERS, or, alternatively, choose a plain fabric to match patterned furnishings, or introduce a pattern into a plain room.

Before choosing a style, consider the purpose for which the light is needed. Frames are available in a wide range of shapes and sizes, some of which shed more light than others. The colour and weight of fabric will also affect the amount of light dispersed. As a general rule, choose fairly light fabrics for best results.

Fabrics

Many types of fabric are suitable, provided they have a certain amount of 'give'. Choose lightweight cotton, lawn, satin, rayon or silk. Broderie anglaise backed with a contrasting lining looks delightful too, particularly when used on a Tiffany shade, and unlined gingham looks cheerful in kitchens.

Small patterns are more successful than large ones, which are difficult to match and wasteful. Pretty floral

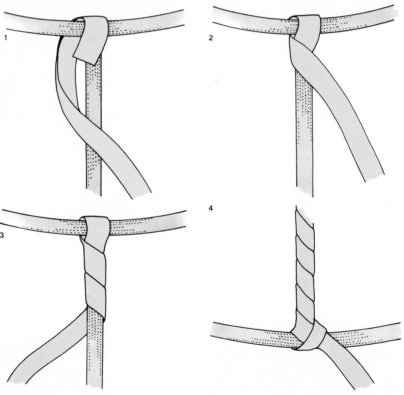

prints, small geometrics and small abstract patterns all work well.

Taping a frame

Before covering the frame with fabric, it is necessary to tape it. This provides a base for stitching and prevents the frame from rusting. Use 1.5cm (½in) wide loosely woven cotton tape, or, if taping a Tiffany shade, use coloured BIAS BINDING to match the lining fabric.

To calculate the length of tape required, allow twice the circumference of the top and bottom rings and twice the length of each strut.

1 Starting at the top of the strut, fold the end of the tape over the top ring.

2 Wind the tape round the vertical strut, taking care to secure the end carefully at the top.

3 Continue winding the tape downwards, making sure that you overlap each twist equally to make an even line of taping. Pull the tape tight so that it cannot unravel when being stitched.

4 Wind the tape in a figure-of-eight round the bottom strut and pull tight. Finish with a few tiny stitches to secure

the taping and cut off close to the stitching.

Bind all vertical struts in the same way and then the top and bottom rings, winding the tape in a figure-of-eight round each join.

A classic fitted shade

These instructions apply to most types of shade where the smallest circumference is the same as the top ring. The fabric is used on the straight of grain, and is pinned and fitted to the frame until a perfect fit is obtained.

To work out the amount of fabric required, measure one strut and add 10cm (4in). Then measure the circumference of the bottom strut and add 12.5cm (5in). You will need a rectangle of fabric this size and the same amount of lining.

Making the outer cover

1 With right sides together, fold the fabric in half. Keeping the straight grain running vertically, pin the fabric to half the frame at the four corners where the side struts join the top and bottom rings.

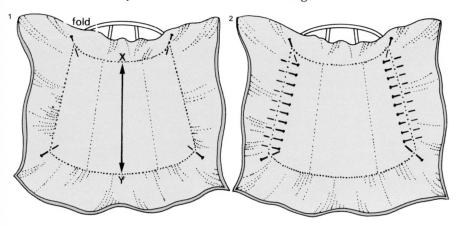

When deciding on a shape for a lampshade it is important to try out a few first, as the wrong shade can ruin the effect of an attractive lamp base.

63

9

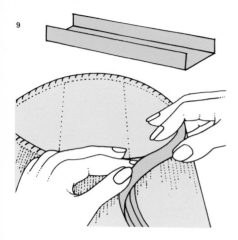

10

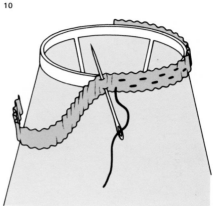

2 Gently stretching the fabric towards the sides, pin it to the two vertical side struts. Place the pins approximately 2.5cm (1in) apart, stretching the fabric and adjusting the pins until the fabric is stretched taut over the frame.

3 Pin the fabric to the top and bottom rings in the same way, gently stretching the fabric to remove all wrinkles. Adjust the pins on the side struts, adding more pins until they are approximately 5mm (¼in) apart.

4 Using a soft pencil, mark two vertical lines from A to B and from C to D along the side struts, extending the lines 1.5cm (½in) beyond the top and bottom rings. These are the stitching lines. Also mark a 1.5cm (½in) horizontal line along the top and bottom rings. Tack the two layers of fabric together approximately 5cm (2in) away from the pins.

5 Remove all pins from the fabric. Using a medium-length stitch and matching sewing thread, stitch along the marked lines from A to B and from C to D. Trim the seam allowances to 5mm (¼in). Cut the fabric open along

the fold line, but do not trim off excess fabric. Press.

6 Turn the cover right side out and slip it over the frame, matching seams to side struts and horizontal marks to top and bottom rings. Pin the fabric to the top and bottom rings, adjusting it so that it fits snugly. Using short lengths of double thread, stitch the cover to the frame. Trim off excess fabric close to the stitching.

Prepare the lining in the same way as the outer cover.

7 Turn the shade upside down. Matching the seams of the lining and the outer cover and the horizontal marks to the top and bottom rings, pin the lining to the rings. Adjust the pins until the lining is stretched taut.

8 Unpick the side seams to accommodate the gimble. Stitch the lining to the frame in the same way as the cover, keeping the stitches to the outside of the rings.

9 Cut a piece of lining fabric 10cm by 2.5cm (4in by 1in) and turn under 5mm (¼in) along each side. Fold the strip in half lengthways, place it underneath the gimble. Stitch it to the frame and trim away excess fabric close to the stitching.

10 Trim the shade with plain bias binding. Carefully spread a small amount of clear adhesive along the turned-under edges. Turning under the raw ends and starting at the seam, apply the binding to the top and bottom of the shade. Take care to cover the stitching.

If you prefer to use braid and a fringe at the bottom, you should stitch these to the shade.

Pleated lampshade

To work out the width of fabric required, measure the bottom circumference and multiply this measurement by three to allow for the pleating. The length required equals the depth of the frame, plus 5cm (2in).

Cut the fabric into strips the required length. Turn under the raw edge at one short end to the width of the pleat. Align the folded edge with one vertical strut and pin to the top and bottom rings. Fold the fabric into pleats along the straight grain of fabric and pin to the bottom ring until you reach the second strut. Pin the pleats to the top ring, gathering them more

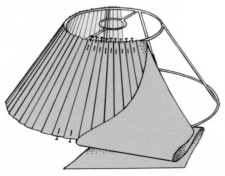

closely than at the bottom. Keep the pleats at right angles to both rings. Stitch the fabric to the rings. Continue in this way, pleating and stitching one section at a time. When it becomes necessary to join the next strip of fabric, turn under the raw end and lap it over the edge of the first strip, so making the next pleat.

When you reach the first pleat, tuck it under the last pleat and finish stitching as before.

Insert lining in the same way as for a fitted shade. Trim the edges.

LIGHTING

Good lighting can add immeasurably to the pleasures of a home, and the installation and use are relatively inexpensive in relation to the benefits.

An enormous choice of light fittings are available today in department stores and electrical shops, from traditional table and standard lights and pendants to modern spotlights and fluorescent tubes, and it is important to consider carefully the options before choosing the style and type of light for a particular purpose.

Wall lights are mainly used for decorative effects, but may provide sufficient light in small areas.

Pendants are used for general as well as decorative effects and are often hung from the centre of the ceiling. However, a low-hanging light in a corner, for example over a table, can look very effective, as can a group of lights hung at different levels. The height of some ceiling lights is adjustable. This type of light is particularly suitable over dining tables.

Table and standard lights throw concentrated pools of light and can be

used either, for example, to read or to sew by or to create atmosphere.

Spotlights are ideal in kitchens and other work areas, as they throw concentrated beams of light in the direction desired. They can be mounted on the wall or ceiling and are also available as table and standard lights.

Fluorescent lighting is available in straight or circular tubes and provides good general lighting in kitchens and utility rooms, but is less desirable in rooms where a decorative light is required.

Track lighting is available to give good specific illumination, for example to paintings or other features. Tracks can be mounted on or suspended from the ceiling.

Cylinder downlighters can be mounted on the ceiling or recessed wholly or partly into it to provide concentrated but concealed lighting. To achieve the desired effect, you may have to experiment with lighting.

LINEN

Linen is a fabric produced from the stem of the flax plant and it often has a rough slub texture. Because of its hardwearing properties, it is commonly used for table linen, and linen union is a very popular furnishing fabric.

The weft of the fabric is regular, and linen is therefore traditionally used for embroidery techniques such as cross stitch, pulled and drawn thread work and other types of counted thread work where the threads of the fabric have to be counted as the design is being worked.

Linen is available in different numbers of threads per centimetre.

LININGS

Curtain lining is often used to protect the main fabric from dirt and direct sunlight and to provide additional insulation. It can be either detachable or sewn in. Detachable linings are made in the same way as unlined curtains and are hooked into the heading tape of the curtain. Slightly less fullness is required for the lining than for the main curtain. The advantage of detachable linings is that they can be removed from the curtains for laundering. Sewn-in linings make the curtains drape better, but they must be dry cleaned, as the fabrics may shrink at different rates.

Materials

Most types of curtain fabric can be lined, except loose, open weaves. Use cotton sateen for the lining. It has a shiny side which repels dirt, and is available in white, cream and a range of colours to tone with your curtain fabric.

Thermal lining can be used instead

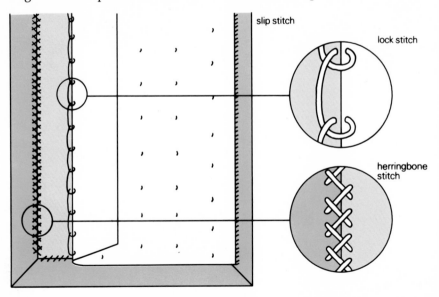

slip stitch

lock stitch

herringbone stitch

of cotton sateen and has an aluminium finish on one side to prevent heat loss in winter while still keeping the room cool in summer.

Estimate the amount of lining fabric in the same way as the main fabric.

Attaching the lining

Cut out and join lengths of the main fabric for each curtain. Turn under the side and bottom hems; pin, tack and herringbone stitch in place. (See Curtains.)

Cut out lengths of lining fabric and join together with open seams. Press seams open and clip into the seam allowances to prevent puckering. Turn under a 10cm (4in) wide double hem along the bottom of each drop; pin, tack and stitch in place by machine.

Lay each curtain out flat with the wrong side uppermost. Place the lining, wrong side down, on top of the curtain 2.5cm (1in) above the hemline. Fold back the lining and LOCKSTITCH to the curtain in vertical lines 30–40cm (12–16in) apart.

Turn under the side edges of the lining, leaving 2.5cm (1in) of the curtain showing. Pin, tack and slip-stitch the lining to the curtain along the sides.

Tack the two layers of fabric together along the top. Measure from the bottom upwards and mark the finished length of the curtain. Turn both edges to the lining side and attach the heading tape in the usual way.

LOCK STITCH

Lock stitch is used to attach lining fabric invisibly to curtains and to prevent the lining from sagging.

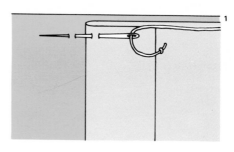

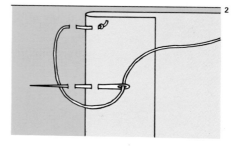

1 Knot the end of a length of thread. Take a tiny stitch from right to left in the lining fabric, then take another tiny stitch directly opposite in the curtain. Pull through needle and thread.

2 Take another stitch 5cm (2in) further down, keeping the thread underneath the needle so as to form a loop. Let the thread remain fairly loose.

LOOSE COVERS

An old sofa or favourite armchair can be given a new lease of life with smart loose covers.

When looking for a fabric, remember that it must be hardwearing, as there is hardly any point in spending hours of work on something that will only last a couple of years. Good-

quality furnishing cotton and linen union are good choices, and they are also the easiest fabrics to work with.

Piping is often used to strengthen the seams and it also acts as a decorative feature, giving the loose covers a more tailored look. It can be made in the same fabric as the covers, or, alternatively, if you are using a patterned fabric, use plain piping in one of the colours of the main fabric. If the loose covers are plain, toning or contrasting piping looks very smart.

In order to be able to remove the loose covers from the armchair when they need to be washed, there is an opening at one back corner and on the underside of each cushion. For closing, use zips or hooks and eyes.

Measuring up

As you measure each part of the armchair, put all the measurements on a chart so that when you look for a fabric you can see how a particular pattern would fall. Remember to allow extra pattern repeats for matching. Be generous in your calculations – any remnants can be used for making matching scatter cushions.

Measure the length and width of each part of the armchair and add 2cm (¾in) to each measurement for seam allowances.

Inside back Measure from the top of the chair (A) to the seat (B) and add 15cm (6in) for the tuck-in allowance.

Seat Measure from the front (C) to the back (B) and add a 15cm (6in) tuck-in allowance at the back and sides.

Facing Measure from C to D.

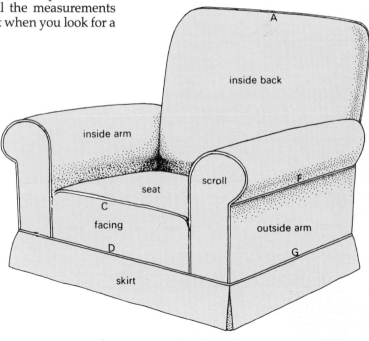

Inside arm Measure from the seat (E) to the bottom of the curve of the outside arm (F). Add a 15cm (6in) tuck-in allowance. Remember that you will need two inside arm pieces.

Outside arm Measure from F to G. Again, two pieces will be needed.

Outside back Measure from the top of the chair (A) to the point where the skirt begins.

Scrolls These can usually be cut out from wastage on the back or arms.

Skirt A finished length of 15cm (6in) looks best on an average size chair. Add 4cm (1½in) for the bottom hem, plus 2cm (¾in) for seam allowances. Measure round the base of the armchair and add 8cm (3¼in) for side hems.

For inverted corner pleats, add 40cm (16in) for each pleat. For box pleats, allow three times the circumference of the base.

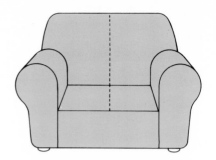

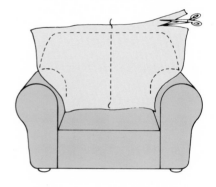

Cushions Measure the top piece of the cushion. You will need two pieces for one cushion. Measure the length and depth of the gusset.

Piping Measure all piping on the existing covers, adding 2cm (¾in) at each join.

Making up

1 Cut out square and rectangular pieces of fabric according to your calculations. Mark each piece with its name either in tailor's chalk on the wrong side of the fabric, or with a pinned piece of paper. Mark the centre

of the back and seat pieces with a line of tacking. Mark the centre of the corresponding parts of the armchair.

2 With the right sides of the fabric towards the armchair, pin the outside and inside back pieces together along the top, taking care to match the centre lines. Also pin each piece to the sides of the armchair. Cut off excess fabric along the top, leaving a 2cm (¾in) seam allowance.

3 Folding all tuck-in allowances back on themselves, pin the seat and back pieces together 2cm (¾in) from the edges.

4 Pin together the inside and outside arm pieces along the bottom of the curve, and the inside arm to the seat. Pin the scroll to the outside arm from the base to the bottom of the curve and to the inside arm to the seat. Trim fabric to 2cm (¾in) and clip curves.

Pin the facing to the seat and to the scroll at each side. Ensure that all seam allowances are trimmed to 2cm (¾in) before removing the cover.

Cut lengths of piping for each seam, adding 2cm (¾in) at each end. Cut the piping cord slightly shorter than the finished seam, leaving the casing strip empty to facilitate the stitching and to prevent the cord from pulling the covers in case it shrinks in the wash.

With raw edges of piping and fabric matching and right sides of fabric facing, tack all the pieces together. Try the cover on the sofa and make any necessary adjustments. Stitch all seams by machine, leaving an opening at one back corner; insert zip.

5 Join strips of fabric to the required length of the skirt. Turn under a 2cm (¾in) wide double hem at each short end and along the bottom. Pleat the skirt as shown, making sure that a full pleat will fall at each side of each corner. (For further instructions on knife pleats, see page 52.) Tack along the top and press to make the crisp pleats. Beginning and ending at the back opening, pin, tack and stitch the skirt to the base of the cover all round.

Make the cushion covers according to the instructions for box cushions on page 37.

Certain chairs look attractive with a heavy fringe round the bottom edge. Finish the chair completely, and fit the fringe last.

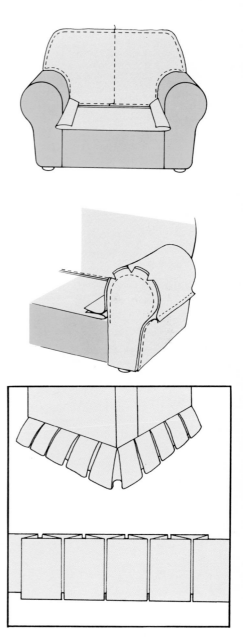

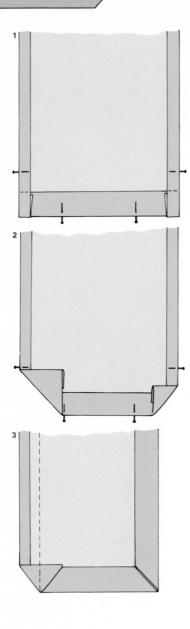

MITRING

Mitred corners give a neat finish to curtains and other soft furnishings and are quite easy to make if a few simple rules are followed.

1 Turn under the total hem allowance along the bottom, for example 15cm (6in), and press, making sure that a visible crease is left in the fabric. Unfold and turn under half the allowance so that the raw edge meets the fold line.

Turn under 1.5cm (½in) down each side and press. Place a pin at the side fold the same distance from the finished hem line as the depth of the first fold. Place a second pin along the bottom fold line at a distance from the side fold twice the width of the side hem, 3.5cm (1½in).

2 To mitre the corner, fold the fabric from pin to pin in a straight line.

3 Remove the pins and turn under the side and bottom hems.

NAP

Fabrics such as brushed denim have a downy, slightly raised surface given to the fabric by a finishing process. When working with fabrics with nap, ensure that all pieces are cut in the same direction.

NEEDLEPOINT

Needlepoint, also known as canvas work, is a special type of embroidery worked on canvas. As the resulting fabric is very hardwearing, it is excellent for soft furnishing such as chair

This sofa is made up of four square cushions decorated in needlepoint in a pattern depicting three skylight scenes. The result is colourful and hardwearing.

seats, stools and cushions. It has been used traditionally for kneelers, altar frontals and firescreens, many of which are regarded as works of art for their beauty and execution.

Materials

Needlepoint is worked on single or double canvas. The size of single canvas is measured by the number of threads per 2.5cm (1in), and that of double canvas by the number of holes or pairs of thread per 2.5cm (1in). Wool, cotton and silk threads are all suitable for needlepoint; the important thing to bear in mind is that the chosen threads match the size of the canvas, which should be evenly covered without looking bulky when the work is finished. Always use a tapestry needle, and match the size to the thickness of the thread.

Some needlepoint stitches tend to pull the canvas out of shape during the course of the stitching. This applies particularly to all diagonal stitches. To prevent unnecessary distortion, it is recommended that a straight-sided embroidery frame be used.

1 Tent stitch is the most common of all needlepoint stitches. It is excellent for details and outlines as well as backgrounds, and is also ideal where subtle shading is required. It covers the canvas evenly and produces a very hardwearing fabric. Although it can be worked in horizontal rows, it is better, if possible, to work it diagonally as this will not distort the canvas as badly.

2 Gobelin filling stitch is also known as brick stitch due to the way in which the stitches are staggered. It is a useful

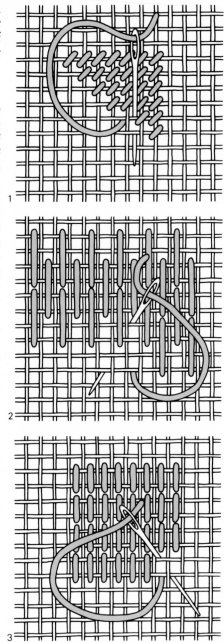

76

background stitch, which can be worked vertically or horizontally, and lends itself well to the mixing of subtle shades and colours. It can be worked over six threads instead of four.

3 Upright Gobelin stitch can be worked vertically or horizontally and can be taken over three or four threads instead of two. As the rows do not overlap, the threads may show through between the stitches and the chosen canvas should therefore resemble the working threads as closely

as possible, so that it forms a toning background.

4 Encroaching Gobelin stitch is excellent for shading effects and is an ideal background stitch, as it produces a smooth, even surface. The canvas should be mounted on a frame when working this stitch, as it can distort the canvas badly. This applies to all slanting stitches.

5 Square mosaic stitch can be worked in one, two or more colours according to the desired effect. Worked in two colours, for example, it can be used to depict patchwork or tiles, whereas in one colour it produces an interesting textural effect.

6 Diagonal mosaic stitch can easily be combined with tent stitch, as it slants in the same direction. It produces a very strong textural effect and when alternate rows are worked in different shades, it resembles brocade. It can either be worked over one and two intersections or over one, two, three and two intersections.

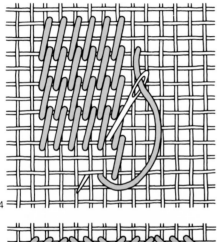

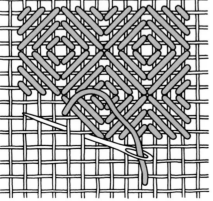

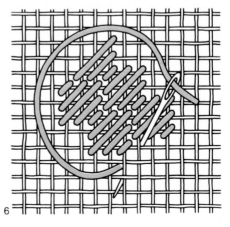

77

PATCHWORK

Patchwork is the art and technique of making use of remnants of fabric by cutting them up into small pieces and stitching them together to produce a completely new fabric. The made-up patchwork piece is treated as a single fabric and can be used for QUILTS and bedcovers, CUSHIONS, table mats and many other soft furnishings.

Old garments such as dresses and blouses as well as remnants can be put to practical use again in patchwork. Choose fabrics which do not fray or stretch. Cotton is ideal, but linen, and silk are suitable too. For best results, ensure that the fabrics for one project are of similar weight.

Patchwork has an opulent look about it, but aside from the work involved, it is very cheap on materials.

Method
Cut out the required number of squares from the selected fabrics, adding 1cm (½in) all round to the finished size for seam allowances. To ensure accuracy, use a template and take care to cut all the pieces on the straight grain of fabric. When all the patches have been cut out, arrange them in a decorative pattern and pile them together strip by strip, so that they will be joined in the correct order.
1 Place two squares with right sides together and raw edges matching.

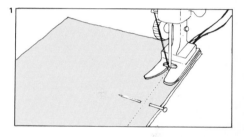

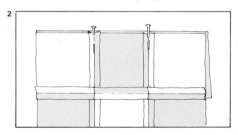

Machine patchwork
Traditionally, all patchwork was done by hand, but today machine patchwork is becoming increasingly popular, as it is both fast and simple to make, and even large articles can be finished in a relatively short time. Squares, rectangles and triangles can be worked together by machine.

Stitch 1cm (½in) from the edge. Keep joining patches in this way until you have finished one pile. Join the patches in the remaining piles in the same way. Press open all seams.
2 With right sides together and stitching 1cm (½in) from the raw edges, join two strips. To ensure that the corners will meet accurately, place a pin through each previous seamline.

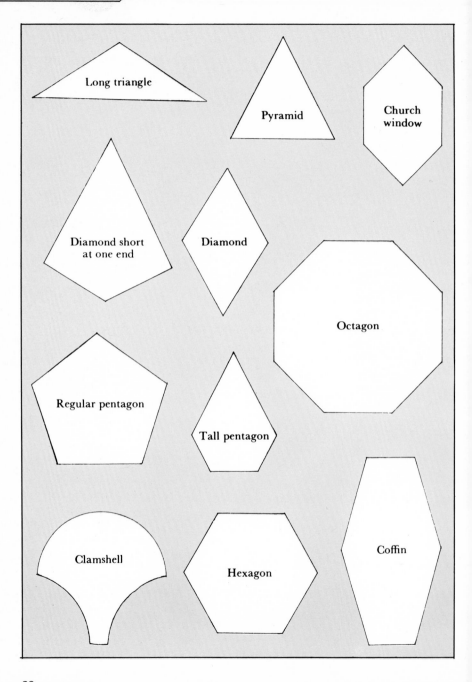

Long triangle

Pyramid

Church window

Diamond short at one end

Diamond

Octagon

Regular pentagon

Tall pentagon

Coffin

Clamshell

Hexagon

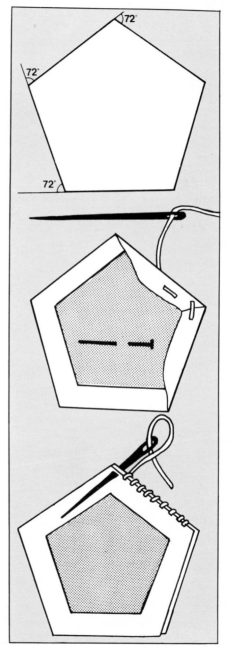

Patchwork by hand

A great variety of patchwork shapes can be stitched together by hand, as can be seen from the diagram below, and intricate patterns created by combining different shapes and mixing plain and patterned fabrics in several shades of one or more colours.

Templates

A template is used to ensure accuracy when cutting out the fabric. Template sets are sold in needlework shops, and consist of one solid template, which is used to cut out the backing paper, and one transparent or window template for cutting out the fabric. It is possible to make your own templates from stiff card, using a scalpel or craft knife.

Method

1 To make a pentagonal template, you need a piece of stiff card, a pencil, a ruler and a protractor.

Draw a horizontal line and mark the desired length of one side of the template (all sides are equal). Using a protractor, draw a second line at 72° to the first and mark off the correct length. Draw a third, fourth and fifth line in the same way to complete the pentagon. Cut out the template. Make a second template 1cm (½in) larger all round.

2 Using the larger template, cut out the required number of fabric patches. Using the smaller template, cut out the same number of backing papers. (This should be fairly firm but not rigid.) Pin a piece of backing paper to the wrong side of each patch, making sure that it is accurately centred. Neatly turn the raw edges over to the paper side and tack in place.

3 When all the patches have been backed, with paper, join them together. Place two patches with right sides together and corners matching exactly. Using matching sewing thread and a fine needle, oversew the two patches together with tiny stitches along one side. Start and finish with a few stitches in the same place to secure the thread.

Log cabin patchwork

This is worked completely differently from other types of patchwork. The fabric is cut into strips of different length, and sewn in rotation around a central fabric square on to a square of backing fabric, for example calico. The finished squares are joined together to make bedcovers and other household articles.

Design

The most characteristic feature of log cabin patchwork is that the fabrics are divided into light and dark and stitched to opposite halves of each square, the diagonal being the dividing line between the light and dark sections.

Materials

Log cabin patchwork can be stitched either by hand or machine. No templates are required and the only materials needed are fabric and thread. Ideally, each strip in one square, or each pair of strips at right angles to each other, should be cut from a different fabric, whereas the squares themselves should be kept looking as similar as possible.

The same types of fabric are used as for ordinary patchwork.

A log cabin patchwork bedcover made in the traditional Straight Furrow design.

Method

Decide on the size of the squares and work out how many are required. The size can be up to 30cm (12in) for a large article such as a bedcover.

Make a paper pattern 5mm (¼in) larger all round than the finished size. Cut out the required number of backing squares from calico or a similar fabric, and work each square in the following way.

1 Press the backing square so that it is free of creases. Fold it in half diagonally in both directions and press again so as to find the centre point.

Cut out a small square following the straight grain of fabric. (Approximately 3cm (1¼in) is a suitable size for an average-size square; the length of one side of the centre square should equal twice the width of each strip.) Place the small square, right side up, on the backing fabric, matching the corners carefully to the diagonal lines. Stitch in place by machine, or by hand with a small running stitch, close to the edge. The raw edges do not need to be turned under, as the straight strips will cover these when they are stitched on.

2 On a piece of paper, draw up the finished size of the centre square and the length and width of the surrounding strips. Four strips of each length are required. Add 5mm (¼in) all round for seam allowances. Cut out all the strips along the straight grain of fabric, and keep them together in groups of the same length and fabric to make the work easier and faster.

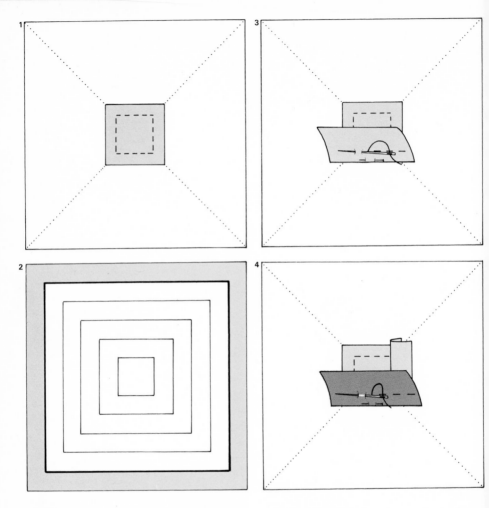

3 Take one of the shortest strips in a dark colour and place, right sides together, on the centre square, matching raw edges along the long edge of the strip and extending the strip equally outside the two edges of the square. Stitch in place 5mm (¼in) from the edge. Turn the strip over so that the right side is uppermost, and hold it in place with a pin.

4 Take another short strip, but in a light colour. Working in a clockwise direction, pin the second strip over the folded end of and at right angles to the first; stitch in place as before.

5 Continue adding strips, keeping two adjacent blocks in light colours and the other two in dark colours.

6 The square is completed when you reach the edges of the backing fabric.

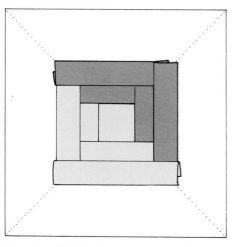

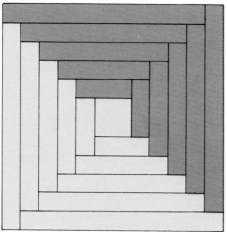

All raw edges will be enclosed except around the outer edges; these will be hidden when the squares are joined together, but must be neatened. The joining can be done by machine as for ordinary square patchwork.

By joining the squares in different ways a variety of geometric patterns can be created. Many of them take their names from the American West, such as Straight Furrow (page 83), Streak O' Lightning and Barn Raising.

PELMETS

Pelmets give a formal finish to curtains and should be designed with the general architecture of the room in mind. Cut a paper pattern to test the intended shape and adjust until a pleasing design has been achieved. The pelmet should be made from the same fabric as the curtains, and be fitted to a pelmet board, which is attached to the top of the window.

Materials

You will need a piece of buckram the same size as the pattern, and the same amount of fabric, interlining and lining, adding 2.5cm (1in) all round for the main fabric, plus extra for matching the pattern if necessary.

Making up

Cut out the buckram according to the pattern. Join widths of interlining if necessary and steam press to the buckram. Trim the interlining, leaving 5mm (¼in) outside the buckram. If necessary, join widths of fabric, matching the pattern carefully. Place the interlined side of buckram on the wrong side of fabric. Fold the fabric towards the buckram and stitch in place by hand.

Place the lining on the buckram, wrong sides together, and turn under all edges of the lining so that it is 5mm (¼in) narrower all round than the buckram. SLIPSTITCH in place.

Attach the pelmet board with small tacks. These can be covered up with a length of braid glued in place with fabric glue.

85

PILLOWCASES

Bed linen made in fabrics which have been carefully selected to complement your bedroom furnishings add a touch of elegance to your home. Pillowcases as well as duvet covers can be as simple or as complicated as you wish. Choose a style which is in keeping with the rest of your décor.

Suitable fabrics

Cotton or cotton/polyester mixtures are the best fabrics for this purpose, as they are hardwearing and available in a wide range of colours and patterns. When making a complete set of bed linen, choose sheeting fabric which is available in wide widths.

Making a simple pillow case

This type of pillowcase is cut in one piece and made slightly larger than the pillow for ease of taking the pillow in and out. It is sewn with FRENCH SEAMS to enclose all raw edges and prevent the fabric from fraying, which would otherwise result from constant washing.

Measure the length and width of your pillow. You will need a piece of fabric the width of which is equal to the pillow width, plus 5cm (2in); the length of the fabric should be twice the pillow length, plus 22cm (8¾in).

Turn under 5mm (¼in) along one short side and then another 1.5cm (½in). Pin, tack and stitch close to the edge. Hem the opposite short edge in the same way, taking 4.5cm (1¾in) for the second turning.

Fold the edge with the narrower hem to the wrong side for 10cm (4in). Bring the opposite edge to meet the first fold. Pin, tack and stitch down

both long sides, 5mm (¼in) from the edges. Turn the case wrong side out and turn the pocket so that it is over the edge with the wider hem. Press the seams so that they fall exactly on the edges. Stitch down each side once more, taking a 1cm (½in) seam allowance. Turn pillowcase right side out.

Making a frilled pillowcase

A frilled pillowcase must be made in two sections, plus the pocket, in order to incorporate the frill.

1 Join strips of fabric to make up a frill twice the length of the pillow circumference by the required width of the frill. Turn under and stitch a narrow

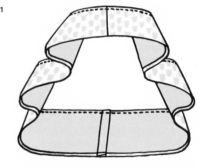

double hem along one long edge and run a double line of GATHERING STITCHES along the opposite edge.

2 Pull up the gathers evenly to make the frill fit round the edges of one section of the case. With right sides together and raw edges matching, pin, tack and stitch the frill to the case, taking a 1.5cm (½in) seam allowance.

Turn under 5mm (¼in) along the long edge of the pocket piece and then another 1.5cm (½in). Stitch close to the edge. Place the pocket, right sides together and raw edges matching, on the trimmed section. Stitch along the short side of the pillowcase, 1.5cm (½in) from the edge.

Hem one short edge of the second section in the same way as the pocket. With right sides of the two main sections together, place the hemmed edge between the first section and the pocket. Stitch along the remaining three sides. Turn the pillowcase right side out.

PIPING

Piping consists of cord covered with fabric, and is used to strengthen seams and produce a decorative finish on LOOSE COVERS, CUSHIONS and other soft furnishings. It can be made in the same fabric as the main item or turned into a design feature by using a different fabric. For example, plain piping in a matching colour looks smart on patterned fabric, whereas patterned piping adds interest to a plain fabric. Piping cord is available in different thicknesses; choose one which is proportionate to the article.

Making piping

1 Cut out bias strips and join to make up the correct length. Place the cord on the wrong side of the bias strip and fold the fabric in half round the cord. Pin, tack with a running stitch and stitch on the machine using the zipper foot, very close to the cord.

2 Place the prepared piping on the right side of the fabric with raw edges matching. Pin, tack and stitch along the first stitching line. Place the two fabrics together, right sides together and piping in between; pin and tack. With the piping section uppermost, machine stitch following the original stitching line.

1

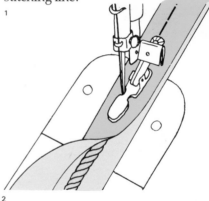

2

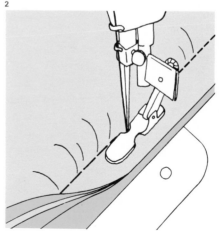

QUILTING

Quilting is the craft of sewing together two or more layers of material with decorative stitching. This produces a relief pattern on the surface which provides the decoration. Quilting was traditionally used for clothes and bedcovers to provide warmth but its uses have now extended greatly.

Fabrics

Suitable fabrics include closely woven cotton, fine wool, cotton and wool mixtures such as Viyella, or lightweight linen. Silks can also be quilted and look exquisite but are more difficult to work with.

When using an intricate quilting pattern, choose a plain fabric which will not interfere with the design. If the quilting is done in a simple geometric pattern, for example diamonds, a fabric with a small pattern may be used.

Certain bold patterns in strong contrasting colours can act as outlines for the quilting. Charming cot quilts can be produced in this way, using a fabric with, for example, stylized animal motifs.

Fillings

The choice of filling depends on the article being made. If it has to be washable, choose polyester wadding, which is available in different weights. For articles which do not require washing, or which may be dry-cleaned, you can also use soft wool fabric, cotton wadding or one or more layers of a flannel-type material.

Equipment

Quilting can be done either by hand or by machine. When quilting by hand, use a sharp or crewel needle and a thread similar in type to the top fabric. Although quilting can be worked in the hand, it is useful to have a large embroidery ring or slate frame, or, if working a full-size quilt, a large quilting frame. This helps to keep the materials taut and the stitching even.

Left: A striking quilted rug consisting of plain and patterned stripes. Some of the plain stripes have additional quilting stitches for a decorative effect.

Below: Joining sections for a quilted rug.

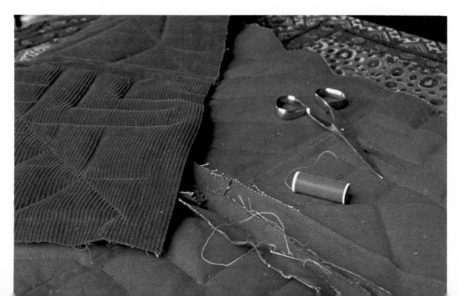

Design

Quilting patterns traditionally consisted of a centre motif, borders with corners and a background filling. These patterns are best worked in a thread which matches the top fabric, as it is the relief which produces the decorative effect, not the stitches. Simple geometric patterns can be treated in the same way, or the quilting lines may be worked, for example, in graduating shades of one or more colours so that the colour effect is as important a design feature as the stitching itself. Completely irregular patterns can be worked either in one or more colours and embroidery can be used to add textural interest and enhance the design. An evening bag in satin, for example, would look

Above: Traditional quilting designs.

exquisite embellished in this way.

When designing a quilting pattern, the main thing to bear in mind is that the stitching lines must not be too close together, nor so far apart that the layers are not held together properly.

Method

1 Cut the top fabric, the wadding and the backing fabric to the same size. Sandwich the wadding between the two fabrics, right sides outwards, and pin and tack all three layers together. The tacking lines should always start from the centre and radiate outwards. When the whole piece has been tacked together, stitch the quilting lines by hand or machine. (The red lines in the

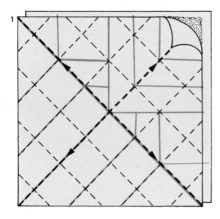

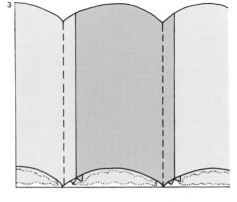

diagram indicate the same quilting lines as are used for the sectioned rug shown on page 91.)

2 When stitching by hand, work a running stitch with a stabbing motion through all layers, going up and down in separate movements so that the thread passes vertically through the materials.

To make up, treat the quilted piece as a single fabric. To neaten the edges, trim the wadding to the required size, turn under the raw edges of the fabrics and stitch together with RUNNING STITCH. Alternatively, finish the edge with bias binding.

Quilted striped rug

Quilted rugs provide an interesting and colourful addition to any room. The rug described here and shown on page 91 consists of strips of fabric in bright colours, plain and patterned, joined together and quilted in parallel

lines at irregular intervals.

Use cotton, corduroy, velvet, wool or felt for the top, wadding for filling and hessian for the backing.

Cut the selected fabrics into strips of required length and width, allowing 1.5cm (½in) on each side for seams. Place the strips with right sides together and raw edges matching; pin, tack and stitch by machine along one long edge, taking a 1.5cm (½in) seam allowance. Join all strips in this way. Press the seams open.

3 Cut the wadding and the hessian to the same size as the top piece. Pin and tack the three layers together in diagonal lines approximately 5cm (2in) apart and at right angles to each other (see diagram). Using matching threads and a long stitch, machine stitch close to the previous stitching lines.

Finish the rug with a contrasting border. Cut 5cm (2in) wide strips along the straight grain of fabric. With right sides together and raw edges matching, pin, tack and stitch one strip to each side of the rug, on the right side, at least 1cm (½in) from the edge. Turn the strips to the back, mitring the corners (see page 16), turn under the raw edges and hemstitch.

Sectioned rug

When making a large rug it is easier to work small sections and join them together afterwards. Use the same types of top fabric and wadding as for the striped rug, but a different backing, for example, lining fabric.

Cut out the required number of top and backing pieces – these should be the same size. Cut the wadding 2cm (¾in) smaller all round. Draw your quilting pattern on the top pieces; tack all layers together as for the striped rug, section by section, and stitch by machine along the marked quilting lines.

With right sides together and stitching through the top layers only, join the sections in rows, taking a 1.5cm (½in) seam allowance.

Trim the seam allowances and press seams open. Join the rows together in the same way.

Place the rug flat on the floor with the backing side upwards. Turn under all raw edges and SLIPSTITCH together. Finish the edge of the rug as desired.

ROMAN BLINDS

Roman blinds are more elegant than ordinary roller blinds and give a smart, tailored look to a window. They can be used on their own or in combination with curtains; they are ideal anywhere where curtains would be too fuzzy or take up too much room, for example at a kitchen window above a sink.

Instead of rolling up, Roman blinds fold up into soft pleats, having rings sewn in vertical rows at the back through which are threaded cords, secured at the bottom rings. The cords are wound round a cleat fixed to the wall by the side of the window.

Fabrics

Choose a closely woven cotton fabric or chintz. Chintz is particularly practical, as it can be wiped down with a damp sponge while still in position.

Plain colours or simple modern designs complement the clean lines of Roman blinds best, whereas pretty florals, for example, are less appropriate. Use cotton sateen for the lining.

Measuring up

First decide whether you want the blind to hang inside or outside the window recess. Measure the width of the window, either including or excluding the window frame; measure the height of the window in the same way to the sill. You will need a length of fabric equal to the height of the window, plus 15cm (6in) for top and bottom hems. The width of the fabric should be equal to the width of the window, plus 12cm (4¾in) for side hems. You need the same amount of lining fabric.

Other materials

The blind is mounted with tacks on a wooden batten which is screwed into position with two L-shaped brackets. The batten should be 5cm (2in) by

Right: This unusually tall window has been elegantly framed with a pair of full-length tie-back curtains. A Roman blind has been added to reduce the height of the window, and is made from a plain fabric that tones with the curtains and the décor of the room.

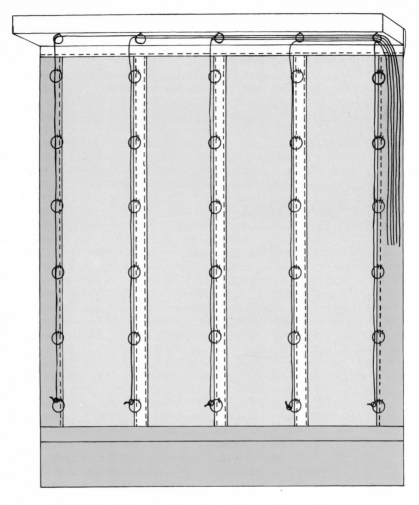

2.5cm (1in) thick and the same length as the width of the finished blind. Another batten, the same length and 2.5cm (1in) by 5mm (¼in) thick, is used to weight the blind and is slotted through the bottom hem. This is called the stretcher batten.

1cm (½in) wide cotton tape is used in vertical rows on the wrong side of the blind as a base for the rings. You will need enough tape to space the rows approximately 30cm (12in) apart from top to bottom. Also buy a length of 3cm (1¼in) wide tape the length of the batten, plus 5cm (2in). Buy the same number of eyelet screws as you have vertical tapes. The brass rings should be spaced 15cm (6in) apart along each strip of the tape.

For pulling up the blind, you will

need nylon cord twice the length of the cotton tape, plus the width of the blind. A cleat is used to anchor the cord when the blind is pulled up.

Making up
Cut the fabric to the required length and join widths if necessary, matching the pattern carefully. Press seams open. Repeat with lining fabric. Place the fabric and the lining, wrong sides together, on a flat surface. Carefully smooth out any creases; you will be working with the two fabrics as if they were one.

Turn under 1cm (½in) down each side and press. Turn under 5cm (2in); press and stitch in place by machine close to the edge. Turn up 1cm (½in) along the bottom hem and then another 10cm (4in); press.

Position two lengths of tape 35cm (14in) in from the edges, measure the distance between these tapes and position the remaining tapes equally spaced approximately 30cm (12in) apart. Tuck in all raw ends under the bottom hem. Stitch all tapes in place along both edges and stitch the bottom hem close to the top edge. Stitch again 2.5cm (1in) further down to form a channel for the stretcher batten.

Starting immediately above the stretcher batten, mark the positions of the rings 15cm (6in) apart. Also place a row of rings down each side hem. Stitch each ring in place firmly by hand with a few tiny stitches.

Turn under the top edge 2.5cm (1in). Turn under the raw ends of the wide cotton tape 2.5cm (1in) and place it along the top of the blind, covering the raw edges of the fabric. Machine stitch along the bottom edge of the tape. Stitch again 1 cm (½in) above the first seamline. To prevent the top of the blind from tilting forward when attached to the batten, catch the top of the tape and the blind by hand every 10cm (4in). Paint the batten to match the wall and screw it into position. Alternatively, cover it in the same fabric as the blind, and secure the fabric with tacks. If using this method, remember to allow for extra fabric in your calculations. Tack the blind, through the lining fabric only, to the batten, spacing the tacks 5cm (2in) apart.

Threading the blind
Position the eyelet screws to the bottom of the batten, exactly in line with the rows of rings. Also mount a cleat at one side of the window. Knot the end of the cord firmly to the bottom ring in the row furthest away from the cleat. Thread it up through all the rings plus all the eyelet screws. Let it hang down on the other side and cut it off in line with the cleat. Repeat with the remaining rows of rings. It is easier to work with the complete length of cord and cut it off as you go along than to try and cut accurate lengths first.

With the cords taut but not pulling, tie the ends together in a knot. Pull up the blind to the desired position and tie a second knot; hook this over the cleat. Run your fingers along each pleat to smooth it into position. Leave the blind pulled up for a couple of days to 'set' the pleats.

Cut the stretcher batten so that it is marginally shorter than the bottom channel, slot it in and slipstitch the openings together so as completely to encase the batten.

97

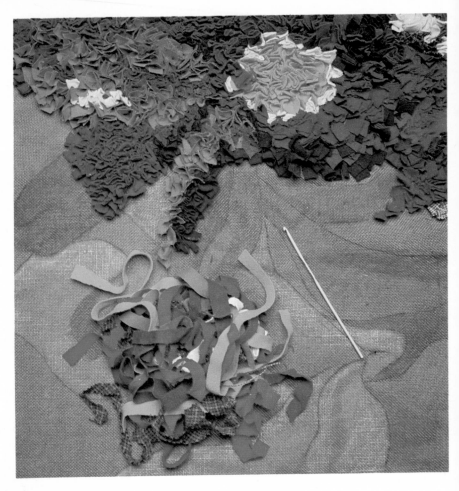

RUGS

Rugs add a splash of colour to a room as well as textural interest. They can be made in many different techniques, for example looping, darning, braiding and needlepoint. Before starting a rug for any particular room, carefully consider the most suitable size and shape, and which type of material would complement the existing furnishings best.

Rag rugs

Rag rugs originated in much the same way as patchwork in that the main principle was to re-use worn out clothes, old furnishings and scraps of fabric left over from dressmaking. Colourful and highly individual designs can be created with rags in this economical way, and they add a personal touch to a home.

It is important to bear in mind that

Above left: This striking looped rug is made from rich, contrasting colours in an abstract, irregular design.

Above and right: This darning-stitch rug, worked on canvas in subtle shades of soft pastels, closely resembles a woven rag rug. A few stripes in a slightly stronger colour dominate the design.

the best results will be achieved if fabrics of similar weight, fibre and weave are used throughout a project. This will ensure that the finished rug will be even, and therefore more hardwearing, and that the textures will blend harmoniously.

Backings

Hessian is the best type of backing for rag rugs, although rug canvas can be used too. If you do use canvas, it must be re-rolled to lie flat before it can be used.

If pieces of hessian need to be joined together in order to make up the required width, overlap the raw edges by approximately 5cm (2in) and pin in place, matching the weave carefully.

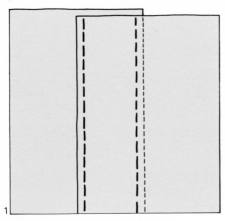

Stitch by hand along each edge of the overlap using a strong thread.
1 Join rug canvas in the same way, overlapping the edges by 2.5cm (1in).

Binding the edges

The edges of the hessian should be neatened with binding before work is started. Cut strips of binding, long

enough to fit each side, plus 5cm (2in) at each end. For a round or oval rug, cut the strips on the cross or bias. With right sides together, stitch the binding to the edges of the hessian. When the rug is finished, trim hessian edge and fold the binding to the wrong side, mitring the corners if necessary. Slip-stitch to the back of the rug.

Darning stitch rug

A loosely woven hessian is the best backing for this type of rug, and the strips should be cut from light or medium weight fabrics to approximately 30–40cm (12–16in) long. Longer strips tend to fray as they are repeatedly pulled through the hessian.

2 Thread a sacking or couching needle with a fabric strip. Bring the needle through to the front and re-insert it 1.5cm (½in) further away to make the first stitch. Pick up two threads of the hessian with the needle and make another long stitch. Continue in this way until you reach the end of the row. Start the second row by working the first stitch half the length.

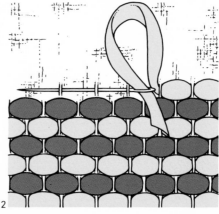

Then continue working long stitches as before. This staggers the rows of stitches. Work the third row in the same way as the first and the fourth in the same way as the second row.

Looped rug

This technique produces a surface of loops, as long or as short as desired. If a tufted finish is preferred, the loops can be cut open.

Cut the fabric into long strips on the bias. Thin knitted fabrics can be used cut 2cm (¾in) wide. Cut thicker fabrics 1.5cm (½in) wide.

3 Hold the end of one strip underneath the hessian. From the front, insert a crochet hook and pull a loop of the strip through to the right side. Decide on the desired depth of the pile and cut a piece of card to this measurement as a guide for all subsequent loops.

The loops should be worked close together, either in rows or round and round to fill in a motif. Leave all the loose ends at the front of the work and start all new strips in the same way as you did the first one.

If rug canvas is used, the back must be coated with latex adhesive to secure the stitches. This is not necessary for hessian.

Braided rugs

Braiding produces thick, hardwearing rugs. Plain or patterned woollen, cotton or synthetic fabrics or heavy rug yarns are suitable; choose one type only for one project.

Cut woven fabrics on the bias and knitted parallel to the selvedge. Heavy to medium weight fabrics should be cut 3cm (1¼in) wide and lightweight fabrics 7.5cm (3in). The raw edges will be turned under and the strips folded in half; the final width will be 2–4cm (¾–1½in) wide. Always use braids of the same thickness throughout an entire project, otherwise the rug will wear unevenly.

Design

Braided rugs can be worked in squares, rectangles, circles or ovals to any size, and the colours and design can be varied endlessly to suit many different décors. Plain fabrics can be used throughout or in combination with patterned fabrics, and the colours can be soft and subtle or bold and contrasting. Arrange all strips in colour groups and plan your design carefully, or use them at random for a speckled effect. Two strong colours and one neutral used in the same braid will produce an arrowhead effect. A gradation of shades is achieved by changing tones as the work proceeds.

Joining strips

1 Place two strips with right sides together and at right angles to each

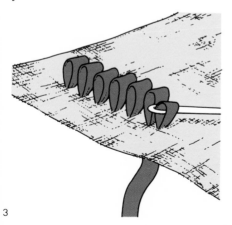

3

Right: This bright, cheerful rug is worked entirely in tent stitch (see Needlepoint), which produces a smooth and very hardwearing surface. Worked in wool, the rug introduces softness as well as colour to the wooden floor.

Rugs can be made in many other needlepoint stitches. For example, make one in monochrome in several different stitches so as to make the changes of texture the predominant design feature.

Below: An oval braided rug in subtle shades of blue and pink. Dark blue has been used to emphasize the oval shape.

other. Stitch diagonally across the corner by hand or machine.

2 Trim the seam allowances and press seams open. Turn under the raw edges along both edges, fold the strip in half lengthways, right sides outwards, and press well.

Continue joining strips of the same fabric in this way. Roll up the strip and secure the end with a pin. Unwind as you work.

Starting to braid

3 Unfold and join two strips of different fabrics on the bias. Trim the seam allowances and press seams open. Place a third strip, wrong sides together, over the join and at right angles to the first two strips. Stitch.

4 Refold the strips and take the third up and over to the front.

5 Secure the end of the strips with a heavy weight, and start braiding by taking the right strip over the centre, left strip over the centre, right strip over the centre, and continue braiding in this way pulling each strip tight to make a firm braid.

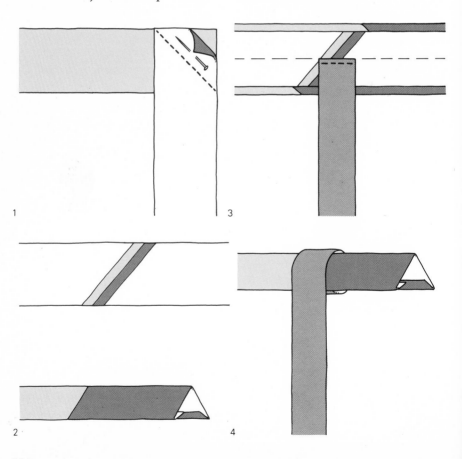

1

2

3

4

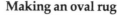

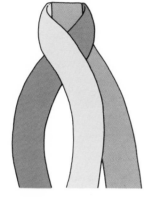

5

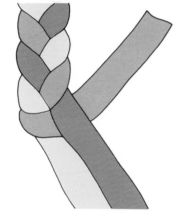

6

Making an oval rug

The width of an oval rug subtracted from its length equals the length of the centre braid.

6 Work the centre braid to the required length and make a round turning by taking the left strip over the centre, left over centre again and then right firmly over the centre.

7 Braid back, lace together with strong thread by taking one stitch in one braid and a second stitch in the adjacent braid. Pull the thread tightly. Continue braiding in a straight line, and lace the braids together as you go along. Secure the strips with a safety-pin while lacing.

RUNNING STITCH

Running stitch was used for stitching seams before the invention of the sewing machine, and is still used in this way for seams which do not get too much strain. It is also used for gathering, easing and working fine tucks.

Working from right to left, weave the needle in and out of the fabric to make small, even stitches.

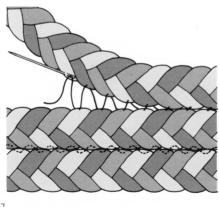

7

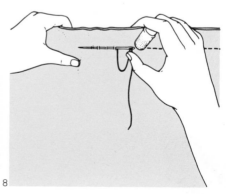

8

105

RUSHWORK

Many pretty chairs and stools have seats woven from rushes. Unfortunately, it is only too common to see these chairs standing outside antique shops with perfect frames and worn-out seats. It is well worth learning to re-seat one yourself.

Preparing the rushes

Rushes are sold in bolts and you will need about threequarters of a bolt to re-seat an average chair. To get the rushes ready for use, soak them in cold water. Make sure that the rushes on the inside of the bundle get a decent soaking, too. Wrap the rushes in an old towel and leave for two to three hours to make them easy to work with. Before starting, wipe the rushes down with a wet cloth. This will clean them and will also get rid of any excess moisture which could cause them to shrink excessively as they dry.

A square chair

Take two rushes and lay them with the thick end of one to the thin end of the other. Tie them securely to the left side rail of the chair using soft string.

1 Take the two rushes in the right hand and twist them to the right, stroking and pulling them so that the two rushes look like one. Pull the rushes firmly down to the front rail at the corner. Pass the rushes under the front rail and up through the chair untwisted. Twist the rushes to the left and then take them over the first twist and down over the left side rail. Now pass the rushes under this side rail and all the way to the right rail untwisted.

Turn the chair round and repeat step **1** in the new left-hand corner. Turn the chair again and repeat until you have worked all corners.

2 Continue with this over and under twisting movement to form the pattern. The first twist in each corner should be to the right and the second one to the left. This cord of twisted rushes shows on top of the seat, but, underneath, the rushes do not need to be twisted.

Keep the diagonal lines that are formed as part of the pattern at 45°

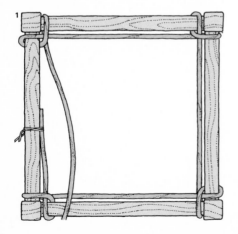

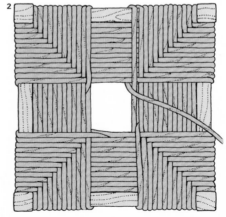

from each corner. Make sure each twisted pair is parallel to the side rails.

It is not necessary to do all the work in one session. When the rushes dry out they will shrink a little and can be pushed closer together for a neater final appearance. Try not to stop work in the middle of a corner, though, and remember to wipe the rushes with a wet cloth before restarting.

When you reach the centre, tie the last rush to the one opposite, underneath the chair.

Joining rushes

Tie the end of the old rush to the new rush with a reef knot. Try to keep all the knots on the untwisted sections between the rails where they will be covered. If two or more joins fall at the same place, stagger them so that the knots do not form a bunch of knots.

Packing

When you have made about a dozen rounds, you will need to pack the chair: turn it over and you will see that pockets have formed, two in each corner. These must be packed with oddments of rush, which can be pushed into the corners to make the padding firm.

A shaped chair

Once you have rushed a square chair seat, you may want to rush one that is wider at the front than the back.

3 Start by tying the rushes to the left rail, as for the square seat, and work round only the front two corners. Tie the rushes to the right rail and cut off any ends. Return to the left rail and start again with new rushes. Work both front corners, then tie off at the right rail again. Continue until the area still to be rushed is exactly square.

4 Tie in once more on the left, but this time work right around the seat as for a square chair. You will gradually cover over the tie in pieces. Finish off as for the square seat.

Several years of bad harvests have made ordinary rushes difficult to get. A good alternative is seagrass, which is more flexible and cleaner to use. It can be bought at most craft shops.

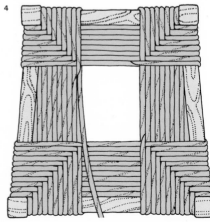

SHEETS

Bed linen, in colours to complement the furnishings, will give your bedroom a coordinated look. Plain colours look best if you have patterned wallpaper, or if you wish to brighten up a plain décor make patterned sheets. Most stores also have a range of fabrics with nursery characters for children.

Sheeting fabric is available in pure cotton or a cotton polyester mix in a choice of plain colours, stripes, checks and floral patterns. By far the best fabric is the cotton and polyester that washes and dries quickly, needs minimal ironing, yet still has the soft quality of pure cotton.

For a double bed you will need to use the widest available sheeting which is 228cm (90in) wide.

To make a fitted sheet

To determine the amount of sheeting, measure the length and width of your mattress. Add the depth of the mattress to both measurements and allow 20cm (8in) all round for tucking in. For a double bed you will also need 1.5m (5ft) of 1cm (½in) wide elastic.

Cut the sheet in one piece and cut the elastic for the corners into four equal lengths. With the right side of the sheet up, pin the points where the four upper corners of the mattress will be. Do this by placing the sheeting on the mattress.

Make a fold (rather like a dart) with the surplus fabric at each corner, and pin from top corner of the mattress to lower corner to fit snugly; taper out the pins by 2cm (¾in) towards the bottom. Tack, then machine corner fold and repeat on other corners. Trim away excess fold fabric and make a

FRENCH SEAM about 1.5cm (½in) in from your first line of stitches.

Adding the elastic

Mark a point 30cm (12in) out in both directions from each corner to indicate where the elastic will go. Make a double hem all round the sheet edge. Machine round edge until you reach the first point marked, 30cm (12in) before the corner. Slide in first piece of elastic and reverse over it to hold in place.

Change to ZIGZAG STITCH and, with the elastic at full stretch, stitch with the double hem folded over. Continue to point marked 30cm (12in) beyond corner and reverse over elastic to secure. Continue to next corner and repeat.

SLIPSTITCH

Slipstitch is a term that occurs frequently in sewing instructions. This almost invisible stitch is used to attach linings and to close faced seams. It is worked from right to left. Secure thread end and bring needle through from back. Pick up a single thread above the fold edge and slip needle into fold for 5mm (⅛in). Bring out needle and pick up a thread above fold; slip needle into fold edge and continue.

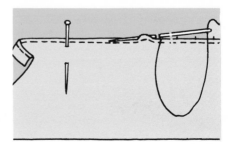

TABLE LINEN

A fresh new tablecloth will brighten up your home and give an old but basically sound table a new lease of life. Cloths are usually square, rectangular or circular, but the style can be varied to suit individual tastes and requirements. They can be made in cotton fabric and finished with a simple hem, in linen embellished with delicate embroidery, or they can be edged with pretty lace taken from an old petticoat or bought in a jumble sale.

Fabrics
For an ordinary tablecloth, choose a hardwearing fabric which hangs well and has a certain crispness, such as cotton or linen. Plain and patterned fabrics are both suitable; gingham, pretty floral prints and small geometric patterns work well, but avoid large one-way designs.

If you wish to embroider the tablecloth, choose a closely woven, plain cotton fabric for free-style embroidery; for cross stitch and other types of counted thread work, choose linen or evenweave cotton.

Edgings
The edges can be finished with a simple hem or with bias binding, which is particularly suitable on round cloths. A short gathered frill, lace or broderie anglaise edging looks pretty, and a scalloped, satin-stitched edge on a round cloth provides an elegant finish.

Making a square tablecloth
Measure the length and width of the table and decide on the overhang. One

Above: Tie-backs can be made in the same fabric as the curtains if these are made in furnishing cotton or chintz. If they are made in a heavier fabric, such as velvet or brocade, use cord and tassel. These are available in many colours and styles. Alternatively, make your own from dressing gown cord.

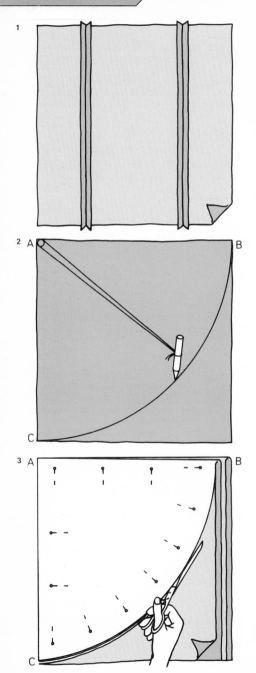

way of doing that is to measure from the top of the table to within 10cm (4in) from a chair seat. You will need a piece of fabric equal to the width of the table, plus twice the overhang, plus 4cm (1¾in) for hems by the length of the table, plus twice the overhang, plus 4cm (1¾in) for hems.

Cut the fabric to the required size. If it is necessary to join widths, make two joins positioning the seams at an equal distance from the centre so as to make them less obtrusive. Press seams open, trim seam allowances to 1cm (½in) and neaten raw edges. Turn under a 1cm (½in) wide double hem all round; pin, tack and stitch close to the edge.

Making a round tablecloth

Round cloths can be either short or floor-length, short cloths being more suitable for a dining-table, whereas long cloths look elegant on smaller tables, for example in halls and bedrooms.

Measure the diameter of the table. Decide on the length of the cloth and measure the overhang accordingly. You will need a square of fabric each side of which is equal to the diameter of the table, plus twice the overhang.

If the diameter of the finished cloth is wider than the selected fabric, you will need two or more widths the same length as the finished diameter. If the fabric has a pattern, allow one extra pattern repeat per extra width for matching.

1 When joining two widths of fabric, cut one piece to the length of the diameter of the finished cloth. Cut the remaining fabric in half lengthways. Matching the pattern carefully, join

one narrow strip to each side of the full width, right sides together and raw edges matching. Pin, tack and stitch, taking a 1.5cm (½in) wide seam allowance. Trim excess fabric from the strips to make a square. Trim seam allowances and neaten raw edges with zigzag stitching.

2 Fold the fabric in quarters, right sides together, and mark with a tailor's tack the corner where the folds meet.

Cut out a square of paper the same size as the folded fabric. Lay the paper on a flat but soft surface and place a drawing-pin to which a piece of string is tied at corner A. Tie a pencil to the opposite end of the string at a distance equal to one side of the square. Keeping the pencil at right angles to the paper, draw an arc from B to C.

3 Place the pattern on the fabric with corner A on top of the tailor's tack and pin in place. Cut out the fabric.

Measure the circumference of the table cloth and prepare the same length of BIAS BINDING. Unfold one edge and with right sides together and raw edges matching, stitch along the fold line. Fold the binding to the wrong side and stitch by hand.

TACKING

Tacking, also known as basting, is used to keep two layers of fabric together while machine stitching. It is a better method than pinning, which may damage the needle.

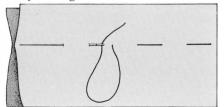

TIE-BACKS

Tie-backs make curtains look more elegant and formal. They can be made in a variety of styles and shapes, and can be finished with piping or bias binding if desired.

Decide on the shape you want and cut out a paper template. To work out the length, place a piece of string round the curtain and pull up the fabric to make it drape gently; measure the length of the string.

For each tie-back you will need a piece of buckram the same size as the the template, a piece of fabric the same size, plus 2.5cm (1in) all round. Buy the same amount of lining (cotton sateen) and interlining as for the main fabric. To attach the tie-back to the wall, you need two rings and one decorative hook.

Making up

Trace the outline of the paper template on the buckram and cut out. Pin the template to the main fabric and cut 2.5cm (1in) from the edge. Cut the lining and interlining to the same size.

Place the interlining on the buckram and steam press to bond them together. Trim the interlining, leaving 2mm (¹⁄₁₂in) extending beyond the edge. Place the interlined side on the wrong side of fabric, fold the fabric over to the buckram and stitch in place by hand. Notch into curved edges of the lining, turn under raw edges 2.5cm (1in) and place the lining, wrong sides together, on the buckram piece. Slipstitch neatly all round to join the lining and the fabric.

Stitch a ring to each end of the tie-back and position the hook on the window frame or wall.

UPHOLSTERY

All a chair often needs to bring it back to life is a new seat. The best introduction to upholstery is to remake the drop-in seat of a dining-chair. These chairs require only minimum work, and a web stretcher and webbing, to make them look like new.

Webbing

First drop the seat out from the chair. Remove the bottoming and top cover. Check the webbing and, if necessary, replace with new. Webbing forms the basis of all upholstery worked on an open frame and is applied in strands which span it in both directions. If just one strand is damaged, the rest of the upholstery wlll sag.

1 Working straight from the roll of woven webbing, turn up the end 2.5cm (1in). Place in position on the back rail of the top of the seat. Insert five tacks in a W formation (three along the edge of the fold, then two slightly in towards the frame).

2 Hold the web stretcher with the handle away from you and insert the webbing in a loop through the slit from underneath. Insert the peg into the loop.

3 Turn the handle towards you and stretch the webbing across to the front of the frame. Press the edge of the stretcher against the side of the frame to give you the leverage to pull the webbing taut.

Tack the webbing again using three tacks in a straight line. Cut off the webbing with 2.5cm (1in) to spare, turn it back over the first tacks and secure with two more tacks to form a W shape. This time the first three tacks will be hidden by the fold. Repeat for the remaining strands, interweaving crossways strands before securing.

4 If you are webbing a seat where the back is narrower than the front, splay the webbing out at the front so that the strands are equally spaced along the front edge.

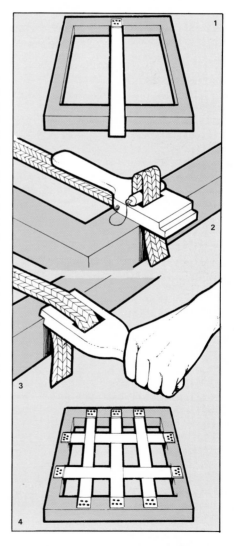

Hessian

To cover the webbing before attaching the padding, cut a rectangle of hessian to the overall size of the seat, plus 2.5cm (1in) all round.

Fold over 1.5cm (½in) on one side of the hessian and, with the fold uppermost, tack it to the back of the seat frame. Strain the hessian tightly to the front of the seat and temporarily secure with three tacks. Repeat this at the sides, keeping the grain of the hessian straight.

Then, working from the centre of each side towards the corners, place tacks about 4cm (1½in) apart. Turn up the raw edges and tack these down.

Padding

Cut a 10cm (4in) deep piece of foam biscuit to 2.5cm (1in) larger all round than the size of the chair seat. Cut four pieces of tape, equal in length to the sides of the foam, plus 2.5cm (1in).

Fold the tape in half lengthways and crease firmly. Glue one side of the folded tape to the outside edge of the foam. When completely dry, place the foam on the hessian, tape side uppermost, and, holding it firmly in position, tack the free edge of the tape to the frame.

Horsehair

If you are working with an old seat where horsehair is to form your padding, a series of twine loops should be made into the hessian to hold the hair in place. Using twine, make stitches about 2.5cm (1in) long all round the inside edge of the seat. The stitches should be loose and form loops large enough to insert two fingers.

Tease out handfuls of hair and push under the loops until tightly packed. Insert more hair into the middle to make a dome. The stuffing should look quite fluffy until you press it with the palm of your hand.

Calico lining

To make a better foundation for the final cover, the foam should be covered with a piece of calico or linen.

Lay the calico flat on your work surface and place the seat, foam side

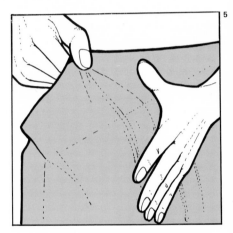

5

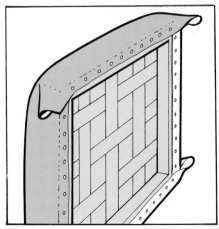

6

down, on top. Bring up the calico on the back edge of the frame and attach through a single thickness of the underside with temporary tacks.

5 Turn the seat so that it is resting on its back edge. Smooth the calico over the padding to the front edge and then smooth it over the frame to the underside.

Starting at the centre of the seat, and working outwards to within 5cm (2in) of the corners, apply temporary tacks

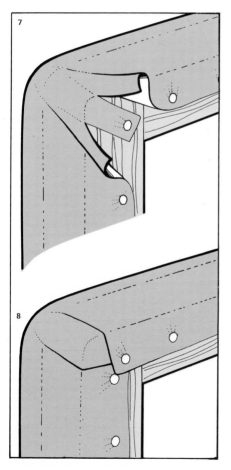

so that the calico is quite taut and there is no looseness when you run your hand across the seat. The foam will flatten out quite a lot as you complete this process.

6 Temporarily tack one side edge in the same way as the back edge, and then tack the other side edge as for the front.

To neaten corners
At the corners, make a double pleat for a smooth, flat finish. Working each corner in turn, pull the calico diagonally over the edge of the frame to the underside. Tack down once in each corner. Fold the fabric into pleats and press the folds firmly with your fingers.

7 Lift up and cut away the excess fabric inside the pleats.

8 Fold under the raw edges and tack the calico to the frame.

Cover fabric
For the main cover choose a fabric that is hardwearing and simple to clean. It should have a firm, close weave and be colour fast.

Fabrics with a smooth finish will keep clean longer than those with a pile or NAP, such as velvet or needlecord, which hold the dust. Our seat was covered in a strong-wearing, satin striped brocade.

Attaching the final cover
To calculate the fabric required, measure the length and width of the seat and allow at least 15cm (6in) extra all round as the fabric has to cover the padding and be turned under the seat frame.

Make centre marks on the base of

1.5cm (½in) of the tacks and replace the seat in its frame.

Overstuffed chairs

You can reupholster overstuffed chairs using foam rubber or the original horsehair.

Removing old materials

Turn the chair upside down and remove the bottoming and top cover. Turn back the right way up and remove any wadding. At this stage you will be able to feel whether the

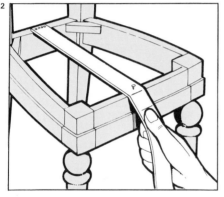

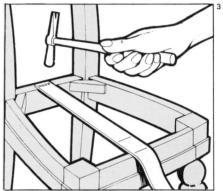

the frame at front and back, and centre marks on front and back edges of the main cover. Place fabric on the work surface with wrong side up. Put the seat, foam side down, in the centre of the fabric and turn up the edges of the fabric to the bottom of the seat frame.

Line up the centre mark on cover and frame and temporarily tack cover into place. When you are sure the cover is well placed, hammer down the tacks at 2.5cm (1in) intervals.

At the corners, make a neat double pleat finish as shown for calico in **7** and **8**. Trim off any excess fabric to within

padding is foam or horsehair.

If you have horsehair stuffing which has lost some of its shape, remove the calico lining to expose a layer of stuffing.

1 Tease out some of the stuffing, reshape and replace it with more horsehair (mostly mixed with other animal hair nowadays) if necessary. Apply new calico and top cover as described for the drop-in seat.

If the horsehair or foam padding is in bad shape, it should probably be replaced, so strip down the chair completely.

119

Rubber webbing

Rubber webbing takes the place of the traditional woven webbing and springs. It is so strong and springy that cross strands are not necessary, although one may be added across the back for extra support.

2 Place the webbing in position on the frame so that the cut end is halfway across the wooden rail. Hammer in four tacks to hold webbing in position.

Rubber webbing should be stretched by one-tenth. Mark the length of the webbing as it spans the seat before stretching. Divide the length into tens and then mark again where the nine-tenth mark falls.

3 Stretch webbing until the nine-tenth mark reaches the front edge and tack down. Cut off any excess webbing near the tacks and repeat for each strand.

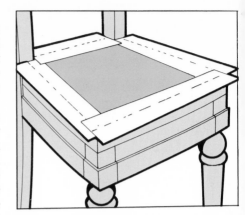

Padding the seat

If the chair has front legs that come up higher than the frame, you can either saw these off level with the rest of the frame, or cut a piece of 2.5cm (1in) thick foam to the size of the seat and glue to the frame to make the surface level.

Foam for padding should be cut to the shape of the seat, plus 2.5cm (1in) all round. Seat grade foam is ideally 7.5–10cm (3–4in) thick. Cut four strips of calico 10cm (4in) wide to fit around the perimeter of the foam, making those for the sides and front long enough to overlap at the corners. The strip for the back should fit between the uprights.

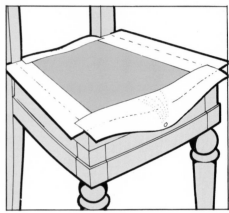

Fold the strips in half lengthways and apply adhesive along the fold line. Mark a 7.5cm (3in) border round the

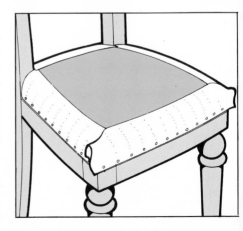

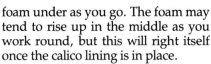

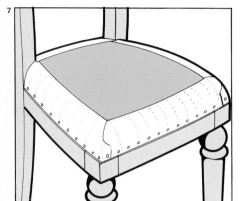

foam under as you go. The foam may tend to rise up in the middle as you work round, but this will right itself once the calico lining is in place.

7 Tack down all sides then pull excess fabric round at the corners and tack in place. Trim off any excess.

Calico lining

Place the calico inner cover over the foam and attach it by tacking down along front, back and sides (in that order), so that tacks are just below that line of tacks which are holding the

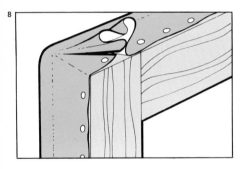

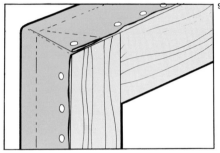

top edge of the foam. When the adhesive is tacky, stick the calico to the foam, keeping the fold level with the edges.

4 Put the foam on the seat and cut diagonally at back corners to accommodate uprights of seat back. Squash the foam to each side of the uprights.

5 Roll under the foam on the front of the chair and pull the calico strip down so that it is flat on the side of the frame and gives a firm rounded edge. Temporarily tack it at the centre. Do not start pulling calico strips down until adhesive is completely dry.

6 Repeat above on the back and sides. Return to the front and add more tacks at 2.5cm (1in) intervals, rolling the

calico strips in place.

At the back uprights, fold back the fabric diagonally away from each upright so that you have a triangular flap of calico. Cut in from the corner of the calico up to the fold. Tuck each piece of calico either side of the upright between the foam and leg and tack down.

Wadding

Cut a piece of wadding to fit over and down the sides of the calico, or long enough to reach below the chair and to pad the edges if the upholstery finishes underneath. Tack in a few places, cutting and overlapping at the corners.

121

Fitting the top cover

Estimate the amount of fabric as you did for the calico lining. Lay the cover over the wadding and apply in exactly the same way as the lining, placing tacks on the underside of the frame or just above the show wood, whatever the style of chair. Once the cover is in place, trim off any excess.

8 If the front corners are square, pull the excess fabric down firmly at the sides and then round to the front and tack down.

9 Fold the excess, which is now on the front, into a pleat which will lie on the corner. Cut away excess fabric from inside the pleat and then tack down.

Finish the underneath of the seat with a piece of black hessian. Cut to size and tack to underneath of chair.

VALANCES

A valance is a very short curtain which is hung from a pelmet rail with curtain hooks. Valances are made by pleating or gathering the material, but the way in which they differ from pelmets is that they are not mounted on to a stiffening agent.

Decide on the depth you want your valance to be, then calculate the amount of fabric necessary in the same way as you would for unlined CURTAINS. For a coordinated look, match the valance to the curtain in both style and fabric, and use the same curtain heading for both.

Gathered valance

Decide how deep you want the valance and allow 1½ times the width of the window. Allow 2.5cm (1in) hems top and bottom and 1.5cm (½in) at each end. If you are making a lining,

cut out the corresponding amount of lining material.

Machine the widths together as necessary. Turn in 2.5cm (1in) hems all round. Machine together the lining and place on top of the main material, wrong sides together, so that the right side of the lining is uppermost. Hem all around, 1.5cm (½in) in from the edge.

At the top edge, machine a length of heading tape the entire length of the pelmet, 2.5cm (1in) down from the top. Turn in the raw edges 1.5cm (½in) at each end. Draw up the cords so that the valance is the correct width and the right position on the rail.

Pleated valance

Make an allowance for the hems, top, bottom and sides, but for a pleated valance allow 2½ times the width of the window.

Pleated valances look better if they are interlined – even if the curtains are not. Join all widths of fabric, lining and interlining. Place interlining on wrong side of main fabric, turn the 2.5cm (1in) turnings in to the wrong side and sew together. Make sure you do not go through to the right side of the valance. Now place the lining on top and SLIPSTITCH in place as for a gathered valance.

Hand sew the French pleats as you would for CURTAINS. With wrong side facing you, place heading tape on back, 2.5cm (1in) down from top of valance. Slipstitch in place and position on hooks.

VELVET

Velvet is an attractive but tricky fabric to work with. The most important thing to understand when using it for home crafts or dressmaking is the NAP. Stroke the surface one way and the surface will feel smooth, stroke it the other way and the surface, or nap, will feel rough. The nap will also change the colour effect of the velvet.

Always use velvet with the nap running up for the best colour effect. It is important when pinning velvet for dressmaking or curtains to make sure that every piece is positioned so that the nap runs in the same direction. Wherever possible, mark with tailor's chalk rather than excessive pinning.

Pressing velvet

To press velvet without causing permanent damage to the pile, always iron on another piece of the same velvet, or use a soft, deep pile towel. When pressing seams open, use a piece of the same velvet as a pressing cloth.

ZIGZAG STITCH

This is a particularly good way to machine fabric edges which may tend to fray. It is also used to strengthen seam edges where a FRENCH SEAM is not used. It may also be used round the edges of motifs in APPLIQUÉ work. Experiment on fabric before working to find the correct stitch length and width. Generally, a fine fabric needs a narrow stitch and a heavier fabric a wide one.

ZIPS

Zips are available in many lengths, weights and colours to match the properties of the fabric.

1 To put in a zip, fold in the seam allowance on both edges of the seam. With the zip fully closed, pin one seam fold to the zip so that the fold line just overlaps the centre of the zip. Pin the other fold in the same way. Any slight overlap will disappear once the stitching pulls the seams back. Tack both folds to the zip fabric and remove pins.

2 Machine stitch or BACKSTITCH parallel to the tacking line, making square corners at the base of the zip. Make sure the needle has gone past the teeth before making the square corner or the needle may break on the metal. Press lightly.

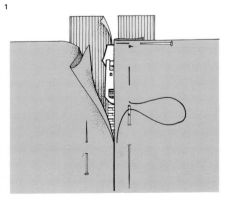

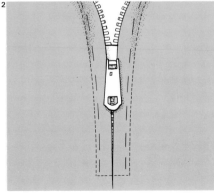

SUPPLIERS

Most of the materials required for the crafts in this book can be found easily at craft shops, department stores or hardware shops throughout the country. However, the list below has been compiled to help readers who may have difficulty in obtaining any particular materials to locate a supplier. Most of the suppliers listed provide a mail order service, but if not they can usually give advice on where their products may be obtained. The list is not comprehensive.

Whilst every effort has been made to ensure that the information given below is correct, suppliers do sometimes move premises or alter their stock. Always check with the supplier before sending an order.

Blind kits

John Lewis,
Oxford Street,
London W1.
Tel: 01-629 7711

J. Barker & Co. Ltd.,
63 Kensington High Street,
London W8.
Tel: 01-937 5432

British Blind and Shutter Association,
First Floor,
251 Brompton Road,
London SW3.
Tel: 01-584 5552

Cane

Deben Craftsmen,
9 St. Peter Street,
Ipswich.
Tel: Ipswich 215042

Dryad Handicrafts,
P.O. Box 38,
Northgates,
Leicester.
Tel: Leicester 50405

Eaton Bag Co., The,
16 Manette Street,
London W1.
Tel: 01-437 9391

Jacobs, Young & Westbury,
Bridge Road,
Haywards Heath,
Sussex.
Tel: Haywards Heath 412411

Wycombe Cane and Rush Works,
Victoria Street,
High Wycombe, Bucks.
Tel: High Wycombe 22610

Craft shops

Dryad Handicrafts,
P.O. Box 38,
Northgates,
Leicester.
Tel: Leicester 50405

Hobby Horse,
15–17 Langton Street,
London SW10.
Tel: 01-351 1913

Northern Handicrafts Ltd.,
Cheapside,
Burnley,
Lancs.
Tel: Burnley 33713

Découpage

Paperchase,
216 Tottenham Court Road,
London W1.
Tel: 01-580 8496

Dyeing
Dylon International Ltd.,
Lower Sydenham,
London SE26 5HD.
Tel: 01-650 4801

General
International Wool Secretariat,
Wool House,
Carlton Gardens,
London SW1
Tel: 01-930 7300

Drycleaning Information Bureau,
178–202 Great Portland Street,
London W1.
Tel: 01-637 7481

Distinctive Trimmings Co. Ltd.,
17 Kensington Church Street,
London W8 4LF.
Tel: 01-937 6174

Rushes
Deben Craftsmen,
9 St. Peter Street,
Ipswich.
Tel: Ipswich 215042

Jacobs, Young & Westbury,
Bridge Road,
Haywards Heath,
Sussex.
Tel: Haywards Heath 412411

Sewing materials
John Lewis,
Oxford Street,
London W1.
Tel: 01-629 7711

The Needlewoman Shop,
146 Regent Street,
London W1.
Tel: 01-734 1727

Specialist fabrics
Felt & Hessian Shop,
34 Greville Street,
London EC1.
Tel: 01-405 6215

Russell Trading Co.,
75 Paradise Street,
Liverpool.
Tel: 051-709 5752

Upholstery
Baxell Grant,
195a Upper Richmond Road,
London SW15.
Tel: 01-788 7423

Buck & Ryan,
Tottenham Court Road,
London W1.
Tel: 01-636 7475

Dangles & Co.,
P.P. Box 12,
4 Hall Lane,
Ashley,
Market Harborough,
Leics. LE16 8HN.
Tel: Medbourne Green 750

Russell Trading Co.,
75 Paradise Street,
Liverpool.
Tel: 051-709 5752

INDEX

Numbers in italics refer to illustrations

Appliqué, 7–8
  bedspread, *6*
  bonding, 8
  fabrics, 7
  padded, 8
  raw edge, 7
  turned edge, 7–8
Armchairs, loose covers
  for, 69–73

Backstitch, 8, 16
Basting (tacking), 113
Bed linen *see* Pillowcases;
  Sheets
Bedspreads:
  appliqué, *6*
  crocheted, 26-7, 28–9
  patchwork, *78–9*
Bias binding, 9
Blanket stitch, 9, 17
Blinds, *10–11*, 12–14, *14*
  fabric, 12
  festoon, 47
  fringes, 50
  roller, 12–14
  Roman, 94–7
  shaped hems, 13–14
Bolsters, 14–15, *15*
Bonding, 8
Borders, 16, *16*
Braided rugs, 101, *102*, 104
Braids, 16
Brick stitch, 76
Broderie anglaise, 35, 60
Buckram, 85, 113
Bump, 52
Buttonhole stitch, 7
Buttons, 17

Calico lining, 116–17
Caning:
  alternative uses, 21
  chairs, 17–21

Canvas:
  blinds, 12
  rug backing, 100
Canvas work
  (needlepoint), 74–7
Chain stitch, 7, 24, 45
Chairs:
  loose covers for, 69–73
  needlepoint seats, 74, *75*
  recaning, 17–21
  rushwork, 106–8
  upholstering, *114*, 115–22
Colour, 22
Colour wheel, *22*
Cord, 23
  on cushions, 23, *23*
  piping, 89
Cotton sateen, 68
Crochet, 24–7
  bedspread, 26–7, 28–9
  chain stitch, 24
  double, 24–5
  finishing off, 25, 27
  slipstitch, 25
  tension, 27
  treble, 25
  working in the round, 25
  yarns and hooks, 27
Crochet hooks, 27, 125
Curtains, 30–3
  crocheted, 28
  fabrics, 30
  headings, 31, *32*
  interlining, 52
  linings, 68–9
  making up, 33
  measuring up, 31–2, *32*
  pelmets, 85
  tie-backs, *95*, *111*, 113
  valances, 122
  weights, 30–1
Cushions, 35–9
  box, 36–7

circles and hexagons, 37
  corded, 23, *23*
  fabrics, 35
  fillings, 49
  lacy, 50, *59*
  loose covers, 72, 73
  making square cover, 22
  patchwork, 35, *38–9*
  piping, 35
  round, scalloped edge, *38*
  scatter, 14, *34–5*
  see also Bolsters; Sag bags

Darning-stitch rugs, *99*,
  100–101
Découpage, 40–1
  cutting out, 40
  motifs, 40
  sanding down, 41
  varnishing, 40–1
  wooden chest, *42*
Domette, 52
Doors, panelled, 21
Duvet covers, 41–3, *42–3*
Duvets, 41
Dyeing, 44
  cold water, 44
  colour guide, 44
  hot water, 44
  French, 44

Embroidery:
  needlepoint, 74–7
  stitches, 45
Embroidery ring, 91

Fabrics:
  appliqué, 7
  blinds, 12
  bolsters, 14
  chair cover, 117
  curtain, 30
  cushion, 35

felt, 46
festoon blinds, 47
interlining, 52
lampshade, 60
linen, 68
lining, 68–9
loose covers, 69, 71
mix-and-match, 34–5
nap, 74
patchwork, 78
pillowcase, 88
quilting, 90
Roman blinds, 94
rug, 101
sheeting, 109
table linen, 111
Fasteners, 46
Felt, 7, 46
Festoon blinds, 47, 47–9
fabric, 47
frills or fringe, 48
threading the cord, 48
Fillings, 49
foam chips, 49
kapok, 49
quilting, 91
synthetic fibre, 49
Flat fell seams, 49
Fluorescent lighting, 67
Foam chips, 49
French dyeing, 44
French seams, 49, 88
Frills:
festoon blinds, 48
pillowcases, 88–9
Fringes, 50
blinds, 48, 50
lampshades, 50, 50
Furniture découpage, 40–
41, 42
see also Chairs

Gathering, 51
Gobelin stitch, 76
encroaching, 77
upright, 77

Headboards, cane, 21

Hemming, 51
Herringbone stitch, 7, 51
Hessian backing, 100, 116
Hook and eye tape, 46
Hooks and eyes, 46
Horsehair, 116

Intarsia (knitting), 56
Interlining, 52, 113
fabrics, 52
curtain, 52

Kapok, 49
Knife pleats, 52
Knitting, 53–8
abbreviations, 56–7
care of, 58
casting off, 56
casting on, 53–4
decreasing and
increasing, 54, 56
intarsia, 56
knit and purl stitches, 54
'liquorice allsorts', 57, 57–
8
Knitting needles, 53, 125

Lace, 58–9
cushion, 59, 59
Lampshade, 60–6
classic fitted, 61
fabrics, 60–1
fringes, 50, 50
making outer cover, 61,
65–6
pleated, 66
taping a frame, 61
Lighting, lights, 66–7
cylinder downlighters, 67
fluorescent, 67
pendants, 66
spotlights, 67
table and standard, 66–7
track, 67
wall, 66
Linen, 12, 68
Linings, 68–9, 113
attaching, 69

detachable, 68
materials, 68–9
sewn-in, 68
thermal, 68–9
Lock stitch, 69
Log cabin patchwork, 82–5
Straight Furrow design,
83, 85
Looped rugs, 98, 101
Loose covers, 69–73
knife pleats, 52
making up, 72–3
measuring up, 72–3

Mitring, 74
Mosaic stitch (square and
diagonal), 77

Nap, 74, 123
Needle, quilting crewel, 91
Needlepoint (canvas
work), 74–7
materials, 76
rugs, 102–3
stitches, 76–7

Patchwork, 78–85
by hand, 81
log cabin, 82, 84–5
machine, 79
Straight Furrow design,
83, 85
templates, 81
Pelmets, 85
Pillowcases, 86–7, 88–9
simple, 88
frilled, 88–9
Piping, 89
on loose covers, 72, 73
Pleated lampshade, 66
Pleated valances, 122
Pleats, knife, 52
Press studs, 46

Quilting, 90–4
designs, 92, 92
equipment, 91
fabrics, 90

fillings, 91
 sectioned, *91*, 94
 striped, *90–1*, *93–4*

Rag rugs, 98
Roller blinds, 12–14
Roman blinds, 94–7
 fabrics, 94
 making up, 97
 materials, 95–7
 measuring up, 94
Rugs, 98–105
 backings, 100
 braided, 101, *102*, 104
 darning stitch, *99*, 100–101
 design, 101
 looped, *98*, 101
 oval, 105
 quilted, *90–1*, *93–4*
 rag, 98, 100
 tent stitch, *102–3*
Running stitch, 105
Rushwork, 106–8
 joining rushes, 108
 packing, 108
 shaped chair, 108
 square chair, 106, 108

Sag bags, 15
 fillings, 49
Satin stitch, 7, 45
Screen, cane, 21
Seagrass, 108
Seams:
 flat fell, 49
 French, 49, *49*
Sheets, 109
 fitted, 109
Silk, 90
Slate frame, 91
Slipstitch, 25, 109
Soft toys, fillings for, 49
Spotlight, 67
Stem stitch, 45
Stitches:
 backstitch, 8
 blanket, 9

brick, 76
 chain, 7, 24, 45
 embroidery, 45
 Gobelin, 76–7
 herringbone, 7, 51
 knitting, 53
 lock, 69
 mosaic, 77
 needlepoint, 76–7
 running, 105
 satin, 7, 45
 slipstitch, 25, 109
 stem, 45
 tent, 76, *102–3*
 zigzag, 7, 123
Stitch ripper, 7
Stools, rushwork, 106
Synthetic fibre fillings, 49

Table linen, *110*, 111–13
 edgings, 111
 fabrics, 111
 round, 112–13
 square, 111–12
Tacking (basting), 113
Tent switch, 76
 rug, *102–3*
Thermal lining, 68–9
Tie-backs, *95*, *111*, 113
Track lighting, 67

Upholstery, *114*, 115–22
 calico lining, 116–17, 121
 chair cover, 117
 hessian, 116
 horsehair, 116
 overstuffed chairs, 119
 padding, 116, 120–1
 removing old materials, 119
 wadding, 121
 webbing, 115

Valances, 122
 gathered, 122
 pleated, 122
Varnishing, 40
Velcro, 46

Velvet, 122–3
 pressing, 123

Wall lights, 66
Webbing, 115
 rubber, 120
Wools/yarns:
 crocheting, 27
 knitting, 53
 rug, 101, *102–3*

Zigzag stitch, 7, 59, 123

PDO 83-277